WHY AM I NOT MARRIED?

INDEPENDENCE, A BLESSING OR A CURSE?

Written by

Sonya Lyons

DEDICATIONS

First and foremost I would like to give thanks to God, for never leaving me nor forsaking me. Even when I left you; This is for your Glory God!! To my mother and father, for the many life lessons that molded and shaped me into the woman I am today. Thank you. I love you. To my children, Sonya Robinson, Shequanna Sonya Lyons and the pain in my butt Shaquan Lyons. I love you.

SPECIAL THANKS

To My Spiritual Mother Prophetess Dr Juanita Bynum; for caring and delivering me from the lowest point in my life. For teaching me about my transition; that it's not about me. There's purpose in my pain. You hold a special place in my heart. I love you.

To My Godmother Gail Juniel-Robbins for being there for me when I was going thru my transition. Your good deeds have not been forgotten. You hold a special place in my heart. I love you.

To Shoneika Moore for your help and support, you are a Gem. Thank you! To Earl and Diane Salik, Denise Jackson, Sheila Hodges. Shequanna Sonya Lyons, Charmaine Darcel, Avery Prince Sr, Jahmenka Nelson, Dante Scott, Novella Nicholson and Kenya Miller for sharing your perceptions and experiences

I hope this book really helps someone.

TABLE OF CONTENTS

INTRODUCTION

In this book I will compare whether it's a Blessing or Curse being independent and how it affects your relationships. I will use my life experiences from being raised as an independent woman to how it has actually affected the success and/or failures of my relationships. Too often you hear stories of strong independent woman asking Why Am I Not Married. They have the success, the independency and the money men love, but they are still single. Are the men just intimidated by women possibly making more money than they are making or having too much control? We will take a look at the different scenarios and I will interview some other men and women to get both perspectives, so they can share their thoughts and experiences on Independency and relationships.

God Knows you like no other

This scripture is what has ministered to me and has gotten me through the lowest points in my life. God knows you and he knows your suffering when no one else does "In the same way, the Spirit helps us in our weakness. We do not know what we ought to pray for, but the Spirit Himself intercedes for us through wordless groans. And He who searches our hearts knows the mind of the Spirit, because the Spirit intercedes for God's people in accordance with the will of God." **(Romans 8:26-27).** The Lord knows us. He knows us better than anyone ever has, or ever will know us. He knows and understands our infirmities, the daily afflictions that trip us up and restrict us. There is comfort in knowing that no matter what we are going through, the Lord understands and is with us as we suffer. You may think, "Nobody knows what I'm going through, nobody feels the pain I'm experiencing." God knows your feelings and frustrations. He's seen the crisis in your soul. There's no hurt that goes unnoticed by God.

Often when we're hurting, we feel very isolated and lonely. "Nobody understands the way I feel; nobody can tell the way I feel; nobody feels the pain." But God knows, and "The LORD is like a father to his children, tender and compassionate to those who fear him." **(Psalms 103:13, NLT).** God; not only sees, He cares! He knows the causes, the reasons, the things that brought you to this point. He understands because he made you, and he sees the hurt in your heart like nobody else can.

He gives us peace thru it all as we already have the victory.

Psalms 139:1-24 NKJV

O Lord , You have searched me and known me. You know my sitting down and my rising up; You understand my thought afar off. You comprehend my path and my lying down, And are acquainted with all my ways. For there is not a word on my tongue, But behold, O Lord , You know it altogether. You have hedged me behind and before, And laid Your hand upon me. Such knowledge is too wonderful for me; It is high, I cannot attain it. Where can I go from Your Spirit? Or where can I flee from Your presence? If I ascend into heaven, You are there; If I make my bed in hell, behold, You are there. If I take the wings of the morning, And dwell in the uttermost parts of the sea, Even there Your hand shall lead me, And Your right hand shall hold me. If I say, "Surely the darkness shall fall on me," Even the night shall be light about me; Indeed, the darkness shall not hide from You, But the night shines as the day; The darkness and the light are both alike to You. For You formed my inward parts; You covered me in my mother's womb. I will praise You, for I am fearfully and wonderfully made; Marvelous are Your works, And that my soul knows very well. My frame was not hidden from You, When I was made in secret, And skillfully wrought in the lowest parts of the earth. Your eyes saw my substance, being yet unformed. And in Your book they all were written, The days fashioned for me, When as yet there were none of them. How precious also are Your thoughts to me, O

God! How great is the sum of them! If I should count them, they would be more in number than the sand; When I awake, I am still with You. Oh, that You would slay the wicked, O God! Depart from me, therefore, you bloodthirsty men. For they speak against You wickedly; Your enemies take Your name in vain. Do I not hate them, O Lord , who hate You? And do I not loathe those who rise up against You? I hate them with perfect hatred; I count them my enemies. Search me, O God, and know my heart; Try me, and know my anxieties; And see if there is any wicked way in me, And lead me in the way everlasting.

David calls upon in adoration of Jehovah the all-knowing God, and he proceeds to adore him by proclaiming one of his peculiar attributes. If we would praise God aright we must draw the matter of our praise from himself -- "O Jehovah, thou hast." No pretended god knows aught (ownership; possession.) of us; but the true God, Jehovah, understands us, and is most intimately acquainted with our persons, nature, and character. How well it is for us to know the God who knows us! The divine knowledge is extremely thorough and searching; it is as if he had searched us, as officers search a man for contraband, or as burglars ransack a house for valuables. The Lord knows all things naturally and as a matter of course, and not by any effort on his part.

Searching ordinarily implies a measure of ignorance which is removed by observation; of course this is not the case with the Lord; but the meaning of this Scripture is, that the Lord knows us as thoroughly as if he had examined us minutely, and had pried into the most secret corners of our being. This infallible knowledge has always existed -- "Thou hast searched me"; and it continues unto this day, since God cannot forget that which he has once known. There never was a time in which we were unknown to God, and there never will be a moment in which we shall be beyond his observation. Note how the Scripture makes his doctrine personal: he saith not, "O God, thou knowest all things"; but, "thou hast known me." It is ever our wisdom to lay truth home to ourselves. How wonderful the contrast between the observer and the observed! God and me! Yet this most intimate connection exists, and therein lies our hope. God knows us inside and out and guess what? He still loves us unconditionally. I hope this blesses you as much as it has blessed me

What Is Success?

Too many people measure how successful they are by how much money they make or the people that they associate with, in my opinion, true success should be measured by how happy you are. To live the lives we truly want and deserve, and not just the lives we settle for. We need a Third Metric; a third measure of success that goes beyond the two metrics of money and power, and consists of four pillars: well-being, wisdom, wonder, and giving. Success isn't about how much money you make. It's about the difference you make in people's lives. Success in life could be defined as the continued expansion of happiness and the progressive realization of worthy goals, success is about relationships and leaving behind a legacy. Success is liking yourself, liking what you do, and liking how you do it. Peace of mind attained only through self-satisfaction in knowing you made the effort to do the best of which you're capable of.

Independence! Is it a blessing or a curse when it comes to everyday relationships or just our perspective on everyday life? Independence: being a state or quality of being independent. Freedom from the control, influence, support, aid or the like of others. Blessing: being a favor or gift bestowed by God, there by bringing happiness or Curse being the cause of evil, misfortune, or trouble. Let's take a look. These are questions every woman that was raised to be independent has asked themselves. It has its pros and cons. We will see it from different perspectives and I will share my personal experiences along with some men and women I have interviewed.

Is our success level determined solely on our independency and drive or is it deemed ok to be the one who will use people to get to what we want or where we want to be? Let's take a look at both scenarios. Independent people naturally tend to be a little more confident in handling issues affecting their lives. Mainly because they are more prepared to take action and do things without having to wait for support or permission from someone else. Being independent therefore means that you will be more likely to try out new things that you desire. For entrepreneurs, this confidence opens your mind to taking bigger risks and unbeaten paths that eventually returns bigger rewards.

Dependent people like those men/women who never have to do anything for themselves because they seem to have different men/women who can fulfill all their needs, at a price of course. They never want for anything or so it seems. Those are Opportunist which derives from the word Opportunism which is the conscious policy and practice of taking advantage of circumstances – with little regard for principles, or with what the consequences are for others.

Opportunist actions are expedient actions guided primarily by self-interested motives. a slick, shady, amoral opportunist who has only one desire: to get through life without a day of labor. I'm not knocking anyone's hustle, believe me. I Just know there will be a point in your life when that's going to get old and God is going to speak to you, tell you to sit yourself down and make you take a look at yourself and what you are doing. You can do it voluntarily or involuntarily, that's when he will sit you down and you won't be able to get up on your own. He will put you in a position where you can only look toward him for help no one else will be able to help you. He does it to all of us when he's trying to get our attention. It's never pleasant when God has to intervene in that way, but it's all done out of his love for us. He only chastises those he loves.

Proverbs 15:31-32

The ear that hears the rebukes of life Will abide among the wise. He who disdains instruction despises his own soul, But he who heeds rebuke gets understanding.

I know you may be saying I don't have any support so I have to do what I have to do because these are the cards I have been dealt for my life. My mother did it, my father did it or they were not capable of taking care of me because of their own demons so I was forced to choose survival. I understand that. I am in no way being judgmental. We as children never ask to be here. In ideal scenarios which most of us lucky ones have experienced, our parents were well-informed enough, with good education and with a good job to feed us and send us to good schools and enroll us in other extracurricular activities and they kept boosting our confidence, kept motivating us and guiding us properly to choose the right path for our career.

On the other hand, In the contrasting scenarios, there are the parents/grandparents who do not know themselves and could not guide their children. Sometimes the abandoned child is living at the mercy of his/her relatives (uncles, aunts) or at some foster home who provide him/her food and may send him/her to some sort of school (not necessarily to the equivalent good school like their own kids' are going) just for namesake but not helping him/her with his school work or guide them properly but that child is managing on his own somehow with the help of some good teacher and friends. Then if this child becomes successful in the future without the proper guidance and support from parents/grandparents/relatives, he would be called a self-made man or woman.

You also have situations where sometimes some kids do odd jobs while studying for their education fees and/or to help their poor parents/guardians with feeding the family. Or they may result to the fast life in the streets for that fast money. Life is a blessing from God and he will sometimes allow us to go thru the most horrific things in life in order to be a testimony for someone else that is lost and confused. Everything we go thru is for his Glory.

There's Purpose in Your Pain. He gives Beauty for Ashes, meaning when you give Him your ashes He, in return, gives you His beauty. If we hold onto our ashes, then we wonder, why hasn't my life changed? Well, you held on to your ashes so He couldn't give you His beauty. There are many people around you who have become successful and rose to the height of their career even though they have seen adversity in their own life in initial years, did hard work and now they are well off. Many could be doctors, engineers, accountants, entrepreneurs, actors; successful politicians like president/prime ministers, scientists, etc. Who around the whole world have achieved the success on their own efforts

What are ashes? Ashes, I believe, are the wounded parts of our lives. Everybody has wounds; everybody has ashes. During the Bible times it was the custom for the people of that day in times of mourning and difficulty to lay in ashes. Just think about that. You've got a problem in your life and you just sit down in a pile of ashes. There is nothing beautiful about ashes. But the scripture says he is going to take your difficult, disgusting, depressing and horrible situation and give you beauty. He is going to pick you up out of the ash pile of life and make something beautiful out of you.

The Hebrew word for ashes is epher and the Hebrew word for beauty is pheer. Just move the e and you have a new word. Just as quickly as it takes for you to move one letter, God is going to turn your sorrow into joy. He speaks and it is already done. You may feel like your life is ugly and insignificant right now. But sometimes things that appear ugly just need the right climate to grow.

There is a Century plant called the "Maguey". It grows for years with great course leaves as thick as two hands put together. It's three inches thick and very long. It puts out sharp thorns and it's just as ugly as can be. The longer it's alive and the more it grows, it just gets uglier

14

all the time. But suddenly it shoots up in just a couple of days and a great shaft tall and thick begins to grow. It decks it's spreading head with thousands of flowers and becomes a beautiful plant.

The possibility of all that fragrant beauty was always in that detestable ugliness. Just as the fragrant beauty of your life is sometimes hidden underneath the insensitive ritual. It is smothered by daily schedules and repetitive grind. Sometimes painful experiences cause beauty to come forth. Isaiah said he will give you beauty for ashes. God knew you would be burnt by life's experiences. But he also knew he could replace that burnt out mess with something beautiful. Like the stories of Job, Daniel, Abraham and Hannah, just to name a few from the bible who suffered adversity and God gave them beauty for their ashes.

Isaiah 61:3 NKJV
To console those who mourn in Zion, To give them beauty for ashes, The oil of joy for mourning, The garment of praise for the spirit of heaviness; That they may be called trees of righteousness, The planting of the Lord , that He may be glorified."
Ecclesiastes 3:11
He hath made everything beautiful in his time:

When Job was a wealthy man living in a land called Uz with his large family and extensive flocks. He was "blameless" and "upright," always careful to avoid doing evil. God boasts to Satan about Job's goodness, but Satan argues that Job is only good because God has blessed him abundantly. So when Job was burnt by life meaning because Satan said Job would not be righteous if his blessings were taken away. God said Satan could take away everything Job had. But not touch his life. Then Satan would see that Job would still be righteous. He burnt the devil because he fell down and praised God. Daniel in the lions den. There was a new king of Babylon. His name was Darius. King Darius chose men to help him. Daniel was their leader. The other men did not like Daniel. They did not want him to be their leader. The men knew Daniel prayed to God. They went to the king. They asked him to make a new law. It said people could not pray to God. The king made the new law. People who did not obey the law would be put in a lions' den. The lions would eat them. Daniel prayed to God three times a day. The wicked men saw Daniel praying. They told the king. The king knew Daniel must be put in the lions' den. The king tried to think of a way to save him. But the law could not be changed. The king told his servants to put Daniel in the lions' den. Daniel prayed and thanked God and he was not touched or eaten by the lions.

Abraham who was about to sacrifice his son; According to the Hebrew Bible, God commands Abraham to offer his son Isaac as a sacrifice. After Isaac is bound to an altar, a messenger from God stops Abraham at the last minute, saying "now I know you fear God." So Abraham was happy and he and his son went and worshipped.

Hannah was barren. When Hannah prayed she was very honest with how she was feeling. She sometimes cried a lot and probably felt like God had forgotten her. But while she was praying she promised God, "Dear God, if you would only look and see how sad I am and remember me, please give me a son. If you would do that for me I will dedicate my son to you for his whole life. "God of course remembered Hannah and gave her a son, and she named him Samuel. Hannah had waited so long for this child and she loved him so much, but she remembered that she made a promise to God. Hannah was an honest woman and when she made a promise she meant it. Again, Hannah had a good attitude and wanted to give Samuel back to God. Hannah kept her promise the day she gave Samuel back to God.

Oil of Joy for mourning.
Oil was used to apply to the face to make the face shine, instead of mourning which disfigures the face and the countenance and makes it unlovely. When in mourning no oil would be applied to the face so that people would know that person was in mourning. The oil of joy is the Holy Ghost. Like a well of living water. Joy; unspeakable and full of glory. Even in hard times JOY. The garment of praise for the spirit of heaviness. Let's talk about this spirit of heaviness. The root of this spirit of heaviness can at times come from: A lack of praise, Bitterness or Being unthankful. The spirit of heaviness will attempt to steal your JOY. Without joy we have the tendency to move into self-pity. For the Bible says:

Psalm 69:20

Reproach hath broken my heart; and I am full of heaviness: and I looked for some to take pity, but there was none; and for comforters, but I found none.

The devil wants you to feel sorry for yourself. He wants you to feel alone and depressed. But don't let him lead you down that pathway. For the Bible says:
Romans 8:28
And we know that all things work together for good to them that love God, to them who are the called according to his purpose.

Listen to what else the bible says:

Isaiah 43:1-7
But now thus saith the LORD that created thee, O Jacob, and he that formed thee, O Israel, Fear not: for I have redeemed thee, I have called thee by thy name; thou art mine.
When thou passest through the waters, I will be with thee; and through the rivers, they shall not overflow thee: when thou walkest through the fire, thou shalt not be burned; neither shall the flame kindle upon thee. For I am the LORD thy God, the Holy One of Israel, thy Saviour: I gave Egypt for thy ransom, Ethiopia and Seba for thee. Since thou wast precious in my sight, thou hast been honorable, and I have loved thee: therefore will I give men for thee, and people for thy life. Fear not: for I am with thee: I will bring thy seed from the east, and gather thee from the west; I will say to the north, Give up; and to the south, Keep not back: bring my sons from far, and

my daughters from the ends of the earth; Even every one that is called by my name: for I have created him for my glory, I have formed him; yea, I have made him.

This is talking about a God that is concerned about you. He loves you.

The Struggle

"The Struggle is Real" an expression used to emphasize the gravity of a frustrating circumstance or hardship, which is often used ironically online in a similar manner to first world problems; also known as "White Whine," that are frustrations and complaints that are only experienced by privileged individuals in wealthy countries. It is typically used as a comedic device to make light of trivial inconveniences.

Now, my Father was a very stern military man so he raised my sisters and I to be independent. Whenever we left the house it didn't matter where we were going or with who, he would always make sure we had our own money in case we needed it to come home or eat. We didn't know it then but we do now he was teaching us independency at a very early age. He would always say you can have anything you want in life if you work hard for it. Never depend on anyone to get anything for you especially a man those were not my words, so don't shoot the messenger. So, there were no silver spoons here. This made a huge impression on me especially coming from a man.

With that always in the back of my mind, I was always determined to do things on my own and never ask a man or anyone for anything. I always felt uncomfortable taking stuff from them when they did try to do for me. I never liked the feeling of owing anyone or being obligated. I always had the attitude like I really don't need you; I can do it myself in all my relationships. I never said that unless you made me mad and by that time I wanted out anyway but overall that's how I felt. I know now that it's ok to allow someone to help if they offer. I just haven't really reached the point where I can ask for help comfortably. It's a pride thing; I pride myself on my own self-sufficiency that I'm still working on.

I believe because I was so strong I tend to get the guys who were both big dreamers with big plans and no money or game talkers or better known as opportunist. I was and still am a very hard worker and independent so they felt stability with me until it would almost drain me dry. I would never let it get me to that point. When I felt like you were becoming more of a liability; a financial obligation, hindrance or disadvantage than an asset; anything valuable or useful, my whole personality would change. I stopped being that crutch for you, giving you the opportunity to move on or change.

I know you hear all the stories about women being gold diggers and using their sexuality to get what they want from the men who are successful and have money. So it appears to others they are the lucky ones, not wanting for anything. Believe it or not there are men out there that do the same thing, they prey on hard working women too these days. They also prey on women with kids because they feel most, not all, but most of them have low self-esteem, especially if they have babies by different men. They think they will accept them just to have someone in their life.

Some single women in those types of situations tend to lose their self-esteem because for some reason society says it's bad for single women to have a lot of kids and not be married. One stereotype is clear as a bell: A single mother is a woman who's careless, selfish, irresponsible, comfortable with a welfare check and dismissive of a dad, but its ok for men to be unmarried and have babies everywhere. Since they don't live with them out of sight out of mind, but because we as woman are responsible and we take care of our kids, they see it as extra baggage or make us feel like we have extra baggage and that we should be honored that they are still willing to take on someone else's burden and be there for us too until they get bored and ready to move on to the next victim.

That's why it's so important to talk about our life experiences. We never know what someone else is going thru. This is only from my experiences so I can't speak on everyone else's opinion and this is not all men, let me add that. There are some good Dads out there that love their kids and want to be there for them whatever the costs but are dealing with hurt baby mothers who use the kids as a tool to get back at them. That's a whole other chapter by itself. We are not talking about them today.

I'm talking about the ones who don't take care of their responsibilities.

That's why we as women have to work extra hard if you don't want to be included in that box of having low self-esteem and you don't want to see yourself settling for the first Tom, Dick and Harry that shows interest in you. Who is able to convince you that he will always be there for you. Knowing deep down inside he's just using you until he gets bored and if the single mothers don't have any female role models in their life to help guide them or give them advice, they will think that what they are going thru is acceptable and is just Life.

No. Life is what you make it. A man is only going to do what you allow him to do. Once, he knows there are some things you will not accept, he will not try that anymore but he will try something else. You just have to be stern and honest as to what's acceptable just as they are in relationships. Hopefully, when someone gives you their testimony and you find out that what they went thru you are going thru right now, they have your attention. Then you focus on how they came out and what can I do to come out of this...

I didn't't really have that woman role model growing up so I always found myself bonding to older women who were strong, independent and successful. I'm still the same way to this day, there's something about seeing a strong confident women making things happen and in control. I believe it's because we have to really go harder than men to be half as successful as some of them are, with more of the knowhow. I always had the determination to succeed and not be labeled a failure despite the circumstances I was faced with. I believe my infatuation with strong independent women comes from the fact I wasn't really close to my mother who I love dearly; so I was always looking for someone who can also fill that void. Who would take me under their wing and show me love.

Now, there's nothing wrong with being a single parent these days because of the times we are living in but it is so much easier and better on our children to be in a two parent household. Our sons need their fathers in their lives to teach them how to be a real man. What do I mean by Real man? A man who is responsible, who knows he is the head of the household and his families well-being is based on his will and determination to provide for them. One; that has a relationship with God, because that's where all his help is going to come from.

Our girls need women role models to teach them how to become wives, there's nothing wrong with being independent but just knowing when she does decide to get married how to humble herself to her God fearing husband who follows Christ. I'm just saying. The problem is we are coming from single parent homes so the cycle continues. Of course I had to learn this the hard way there was no one there to teach me, that's why role models are so important and you have to be open and willing to listen to correction or advice. You know how we get sometimes when we think we have all the answers and our life is not going to turn out like our parents..

The Early Years

Growing up my father was very strict on us. He was a no nonsense type of guy. He would get up at the crack of dawn on his days off, sit in his favorite chair and read the newspaper. I believe he was hard on us because all he had was girls. He was a very hard worker and a good provider even though he was frugal and he had an 850 Fico credit score .He knew how to save money. There had to be a very good reason for him to come out of pocket. I remember he would go in another room when we needed money for something just so we couldn't see the stack he would pull out. We used to laugh at him in secret because we knew what he was doing. He was serious about his paper. I was the only one bold enough to ask "Daddy, why do you always go to the bathroom or another room when we ask you for money". Till this day I never got an answer but I already knew. I remember he used to have a back pack filled with nothing but quarters just because. No dimes, nickels or pennies; just quarters. Every day when he came home from work he would dump his change in that back pack. It was heavy as a brick. He would hide it in his closet and when my sisters and I found it we were never broke. He never knew we were taking some of it because that's how full it was. So he never missed it. Sorry daddy.

When It came to committed relationships I believe he was trying to protect us from guys like him. He taught us to love with our minds and not with our hearts and to never give a man complete control; but of course me being that sucker for love and born on his birthday I think I got the short end of the deal. Always giving my all in a relationship. Don't get me wrong I'm not quick to fall in love but when I do I love hard. I believe I'm a hopeless romantic: A person who is in love with love. We believe in fairy tales and love. Not to be confused as stalkers or creepy because that's not what a hopeless romantic is. All hopeless romantics are idealists, the sentimental dreamers, the imaginative and the fanciful when you get to know us. We make love look like an art form with all the romantic things we will do for our special someone. Someone; that's more in love with the act of being in love than really being in love with that person, one who likes long walks on the beach, candlelight dinners, etc.

This was a learned behavior from reading all those romance novels growing up and my experiences with relationships. I'm working on the concept of being in love with the person now and not just love. I'm not trying to be bitter, I'm just being cautious with my heart. I think that's well deserving. Just guarding my heart and trying to keep it pure. I'm not afraid of commitment like my father was. I didn't't get that gene. I'm just not going to give it away anymore to just anyone. I need to know that you are really there for me unconditionally, thru the good and the bad.

Ok, I have trust issues. There I said it. Trust Issues: A total lack of intimacy or friendships due to mistrust. The mistrust that usually interferes with one's primary relationship. Several intensely dramatic and stormy relationships in a row or at once. Also, racing thoughts of suspicion or anxiety about friends and family. I'm working on that too. I will give you the benefit of the doubt in the beginning. You will have to be the one that breaks my trust. I won't automatically just throw you in that category.

My father was in the military and he travelled a lot before he had us so he used to tell us stories of all the woman he dated from all nationalities while being stationed all over the world. He said these women would say they loved him and wanted to marry him but that was the farthest from his mind. So; that word never really meant anything to him when it came to relationships. That's why he tried to make us hard. He was the type of man that would tell you the truth about anything whether it hurt your feelings or not. He would apologize sometimes later when he realized it hurt you but he always kept it real.

He was so overprotective. I remember when I was dating this older guy who lived in our condo; he was in the military so I didn't get to see him much. I don't even know if you could call it dating because I didn't see him a lot but he was FINE! He was light skinned, curly haired and bowlegged. He would have been my first if we were ever given the time and opportunity. I'm just saying. He came home on a break one day and came to see about me. My father answered the door and said who are you? He told him who he was and asked if I was there. My father wouldn't even let him finish, he said you don't just show up at my house asking for my daughter you at least call first and slammed the door. I believe my father saw himself in my date and recognized he was military and was like, *Umm heck no*. It's something about a clean cut man that dresses nice and smells good, all the time. So when I realized it was for me; being the spoiled daddy's girl that I was, I yelled at my dad and ran after him. See his bark was worse than his bite when it came to his girls but let someone else even look at us wrong he was ready to fight.

Another example In New York when the weather is nice everyone is outside on the block even the older people just sitting around drinking, playing cards and just having a good time. So i was playing outside on the block and this man drove up to where I was. I had to be about 15 at the time. I don't remember what he said to me but all my father needed to see was this grown man talking to his baby he ran over to me so fast and tried to pull this man out of his car The man was so scared he sped off. I can still see the visual until this very day; my dad had his dukes up and was pulling at this man to get out the car. I laugh about it now my dad didn't play.

I think my dad knew because he was a ladies man that some of it would come back to hurt his girls so he wanted us to have tough skin. He wanted us to be able to spot the jokers from a mile away like he could. That way we wouldn't allow that to happen to us. My father was not the type of dad that would sit you down and have those conversations with you. He was more of the father that talked at you and told you what you better not do or else. So, we could always tell when he talked by his tone how upset he was if he was at all. I can't speak for the rest of my sisters but my Dad and I had a special bond. I didn't always like the things he said or did sometimes but I loved him and I miss him every day. Rest in Heaven Daddy.

On another note, these days it seems like we are raising our girls to be strong independent woman who can do for themselves and we are pampering our boys to where they turn out to be mama's boys looking for the same mama figure in a wife. So, Instead of finding strong men to lead us we as women are leading. Which causes some of our men to look elsewhere for someone more passive; accepting or allowing what happens or what others do, without active response or resistance. If they are not into strong and independent women.

I never understood that from some men because if you came from a strong independent woman how could you not want the same? You want someone passive and totally dependent on you. I call that needy. Don't get me wrong I know all about being submissive to your husband, but I also believe in every relationship both parties should give 100% of themselves not 50/50. That way there's no room for someone feeling overwhelmed, needy or that they are being taken advantage of. With that type of drive from both parties the sky is the limit on what you can accomplish together.

In a marriage where each person is contributing equally and honestly there should be some sort of dependence on both sides, the two need each other for different things. Mainly in each person's area of weakness. Where I am weak, You make me strong. Creating a balance for one another. You can be married and still keep somewhat of your independence. You can have joint accounts to share household expenses and still have your own individual accounts, so if you want to have a girl's night or you see a purse you want to buy you don't have to ask since it's your money you can do it. Even in a marriage I believe your spouse can't totally complete you, this comes from your relationship with God, and your spouse is just the icing on the cake.

In any new relationship a person is more in love or intrigued with what they don't know about the other person, the suspense of not knowing and getting to know each other is what's intriguing. The challenge of getting to know or conquer the other person is what you are really attracted to. The real test is after the suspense is gone and you know everything there is to know about the other person. Are you still intrigued or bored now? That's where Volitional love comes to play; a Choice or decision made by the willingness to love.

How can you tell if it's really volitional love? The other person can make you so mad or can do something to you so horrific, after you tell them and they apologize you decide that you still want to stay around and be committed to them. You are not ready to throw in the towel. Not like this microwave generation we live in now where no one wants to work on anything, they just move on to the next one. Happiness comes from within it doesn't come from your mate. So if you are already happy and complete in Christ when your mate falls short you are still complete.

Innocence

Young love while still in primary school. Young love, can be the most innocent relationships. They start off just being sweet to each other hanging out, holding hands, cuddling and little kisses. No making out, fooling around, sleeping together or anything like that at first; just innocent. The most innocent relationships, at least from my experience is your first love or should I say puppy love. When you both are young and there are no scars from past hurts because everything is new. You feel like together y'all can take on the world and you have all the answers. While still living in your parents' house. That tickles me to this day just thinking about it.

I met my first love in high school. I was one of those pretty nerds that always got good grades. I was in every program there was growing up from piano lessons to studying with the Dance Theatre of Harlem and LaRocque Bey Dancers to every beauty pageant there was. Yes, that was my life. So I really didn't have time to think about a boyfriend. The only time I could have spent with one would have to be at school.

My first love was a pretty boy, very athletic and he could dress. I didn't know that even mattered to me until we started talking and he would always smell good. I mean all the time. In high school mind you!. I should have run right then. *Chuckles* I was young, sheltered and still a virgin so I was intrigued by how different he was. He was the baby out of 7 brothers and sisters so he was way more advanced than I was. He taught me everything he knew at that time about love and relationships. We were inseparable, before long I was cutting my last period class just so we can have more time together. He was a very good boyfriend from what little I knew about relationships and I was happy. We would dress alike. We had matching shearling coats with the hats and gloves to match. Thinking about it now that was lame but cute.

He would pick me up from work after school. (See I always had a job even in high school) I had expensive taste and didn't like asking my parents for money so I made my own and bought myself whatever I wanted. So, years went by and we became real serious. We were Frick and Frack, you didn't see one without the other. At that point and time when you're young you both have dreams and aspirations and are willing to help each other become successful. We would talk about getting married, having our own businesses, the white picket fence and having a family. All in that order.

Reality kicks in when you graduate, you get your own place together and then here comes baby that makes three. Not saying you no longer have those dreams and aspirations, it just makes it harder and some things will have to be put on hold. Life has a way of waking you up out of your fairytale and making your reality precedent; something that precedes, or comes before. So depending on how determined you are to succeed, you work even harder and don't let your current situation keep you in a place you know is not your destiny. I guess you can say Sonya matured a lot after having her baby.

Needless to say, my first love didn't. He was so accustomed to being babied and not really having to be held responsible for his actions, because mommy and daddy were always there to bail him out; you start to see things differently. I loved his parents; they were always so loving and caring. They always treated me like their very own. Heck, they babied me too so I could see how you could get used to that. He was the baby out of 7 kids so that explains it.

His answer to help our situation so we wouldn't have to struggle was to move back in with our parents so we can save money .His parents already had a house full. My pride stepped in and I saw that as a step backwards so I definitely wasn't going to do that. I remembered when we told my father we were going to get married, my father grilled him with stuff like you haven't even lived yet you not ready to get married. A ring doesn't mean anything I bought every woman I was with a ring. My father met his match, my fiancé stood up to him while still being respectful. He had a good comeback for every question. He wasn't intimidated by him and from this day my sisters and I talk about how he was the only guy who stood up to my father, because he was cool like that. Everyone else would be too scared and run away.

So with that being said instead of me wanting to run back home to mommy and daddy, to show my dad he was right, since i was raised to be independent I set out to work even harder with a baby. While my baby's father moves back home where he doesn't have to pay bills. His only job was to stay fly and he was always able to buy himself the finer things. He was always sharp. Taylor made suits, all different type of fur coats. As I can recall now I think his only passion was to dress in the finer things but he never had a 9-5. Everyone is not able. *chuckle chuckle*

So from the very beginning my perception changed the way I looked at life but not my perseverance or determination. I was a single mother with a full time Job and going to College full time now. Sleep wasn't something I got a lot of. I can remember times coming home from work 2 in the morning riding the train in New York City, falling asleep but God always managed to wake me up right before it was time for me to get off. He was watching over me even then. He never allowed any harm to come to me and yet I never thanked him at that time. Thank You Jesus!

It was a trying 4 years but the feeling of relief and accomplishment that I felt when I graduated was worth it. I don't regret doing what I did and the decisions I made to keep pushing forward, because to this day my first love never left the nest. I also love the fact that my children witnessed the fact their single mother was independent, she worked hard, finished college and they never wanted for anything. I do regret all the time I spent away from them while trying to provide for them, so I would try to make it up with summer vacations.

Reality Sets In

After Graduation all the good jobs came, I was able to provide for me and my daughter the way I wanted to. She never wanted for anything. Along with the good jobs came the guys. I guess there are some men that are attracted to independent women. They loved seeing a woman doing for herself and happy but for some reason I always got the ones that were only looking for stability or a come up and not the ones who were raised to provide the stability. I guess you can say I was a bum magnet. If there was a fly, good looking bum out there I was attracted him. They would get me every time with the clean cuts, nice clothes and always smelling good, but they never had a real job. Shaking my head.

So for a long time I thought that's how it was. Was there something in me that I didn't realize that was attracting these types of men? Yes, there had to be. Whenever you keep attracting the same type of people it's because there's something in your spirit that draws their spirit, so that's when you ask God to show you everything about yourself and what needs to be changed. At that time. Not really understanding that according to the Bible and how things are supposed to work, a man is supposed to be the provider and we are his help mates. I didn't really care as long as I wasn't alone. I was proud of my accomplishments but not my choices in men. The sad thing about it is all my relationships lasted for years, the shortest relationship I had was I think 3 yrs. Time you can't get back.

Now, I was raised in the church. Where we had to memorize all 66 books of the Bible, we recited various scriptures for church programs but were never really taught about the Holy Spirit. We were in every play, the choir, Sunday school programs but when you're young and you read the Bible you lack true understanding on your own; there was no one there really to teach me. So for me it was just something we had to do; maybe my Spirit wasn't ready to be awakened because I see kids now that are really filled with the Holy Ghost. You can tell if it was taught behavior or if they are really feeling the Holy Spirit. Maybe it was the type of church I was in. They didn't believe in praising God and making a lot of noise. I'm glad I was raised in the church though because it has molded me and shaped me into the God Fearing woman I am today.

I didn't really experience the Holy Spirit though until I was living on my own and my best friend and I who we have been friends since we were 3 years old were drawn to a Baptist Church where they were loud and always looked like they were having a good time. The Church I grew up in was more Pentecostal if you breathed too loud the whole congregation would look at you funny like you done lost your mind. So this was very different for me. It became addictive to me and it seemed like my Soul was waking up. I remember before my bestie and I were introduced to that church we would just be sitting outside on the stoop of her building every day after work. That's what New Yorkers did when they got off work they would just chill outside. Every day there was a lady we called Sister J who was always quoting scriptures. When she came home from, I guess work she always had to walk past my besties building and every day she passed us she was always trying to tell us about Jesus; she was so serious. We never took her serious because she was always drunk, you could smell it on her but she knew the word.

Everyone has their own demons they are dealing with and God will use anyone. We would always laugh at her when we saw her coming and it never failed she always stopped to talk to us. It wasn't until my best friends Godmother who she lived with, who also became my God mother because she was like a mother to us both and we called her Mama, got sick and she had to be rushed to the hospital. Mama's window was right in the front of the building on the first floor. She was in the mist of everything going on and she was always sitting at that window while we were sitting on the stoop every day.

So when she never made it home from the hospital we felt empty and we were devastated. I remember the last day we were going to the hospital to see her, I fell asleep on her bed. I dreamed that she had come to me as a young child and she was laying next to me on the bed. Needless to say I jumped up, told my best friend about but I wasn't afraid because she came in peace. We didn't know at the time she had died.

We found out when we went to the hospital they told us and allowed us to view her body one last time. After that I realized that was her Spirit that came to me. It was a very painful time for us both but more for my best friend because Mama was her family and now she was all alone in that huge apt where we witnessed Mama's husband die of a heart attack years earlier and now, Mama was gone. I'm not going to lie we were afraid to stay in that apt. My apt was down the street but it was no way as big as hers, so being the best friend that I was I would stay over and we would all sleep in the same room babies and all scared together.

Since Mama was no longer there it was getting hard financially for both of us and Sister J would come and still minister to us and also tell us where we could get assistance like food and stuff from churches. We were still babies ourselves just graduating high school and we both had a baby so we welcomed the advice. There we were introduced to that Baptist Church. I remember when we used to have all night prayer. I literally would be up all night praying with a church full of people. So thus I was introduced to the prayer life. I remember the first time I went to all night prayer I was crying, throwing up and I felt a presence that I never felt before while I was tarrying which is constantly worshipping God. When I felt that presence on me I got scared and stopped. Not, understanding that I was being visited by the Holy Spirit, that is what I was tarrying for.

Until this day I have not felt that presence again like I did that night and I wish I had not stopped. You see another example of how God brings people in your life for a reason even if we don't understand it at the time. I was serious about my new found religion and where it was taking me but then I got side tracked. Guess how? A man. That's what the enemy does. I was still a babe in Christ so I fell for it. I wasn't complete or happy within myself so I was looking for love in a man to complete me and not in God.

Let me not give the enemy all the credit, I was trying to fill a void and I thought a man was the answer. Let me take responsibility for my actions. I was one of those women that always had options but only a very few would get my attention. If you got my attention then there had to be something special about you, so I would jump on that ride and ride it until the wheels fell off. I know now that was destined to fail. How can you choose a man over God? I'm not saying that I had to but I made the decision to stop going to church. If I were God I would be mad too. We serve a jealous God. While I was searching for my happiness I was blessed with my children who I love dearly so all wasn't completely lost.

Love Is Blind

Love is blind meaning; if you love someone, you cannot see any faults in that person. Now, my next close call was with my son's father. How do you work in Corporate America and your Fiancé/sons father is a street hustler that can't stay out of trouble. They say opposites attract but I knew better. I was looking for someone to fill that void in me. There's that cycle again trying to find happiness in someone else because you are not happy within yourself. I met him thru my sister she was dating his brother, so that was convenient. They lived in the projects. There's nothing wrong with that because I had a lot of friends that lived in the projects but they didn't stay there. These guys were thugs I mean straight up thugs. I guess that was the era where ruff necks were in. Chuckle! Chuckle! What was I thinking?

The things we did with them were stuff you would see in the movies though like for example; we would drive up and down 42nd street and Broadway. Now for all my non New Yorkers that is one of the busiest streets in Manhattan. Just picture those commercials you see where they have hundreds of people walking down the street during the day with their nice suits on. We would drive down 42nd street with a super soaker full of water. For those not familiar with the super soakers it's a giant water gun that holds gallons of water and when you shoot it the water comes out like a water hose. We would drive down the street squirting all the people who were stopped at the corner waiting to cross the street. These people would be dressed in their suits and dresses from work and they would be drenched. It's not funny now but at the time it was hilarious because most of them didn't even know where the water was coming from. They would look up in the sky but the sun would be shining bright so they were clueless. One time we squirted this yellow cab driver. Now we all know back then yellow cab drivers were crazy. He started yelling at us in a different language and started chasing us down the street. It was a high speed chase but eventually he backed down. Needless to say the relationship I had with him was always like that never a dull moment. We were young and immature.

His mother couldn't stand me though and that was a first for me because I always bonded with the mothers. She was one of those mothers that would actually smoke with her sons. I never smoked or drank because it just wasn't my desire too. I had friends that would and would always try to convince me but I was a leader not a follower so instead they would try to give me a contact. *Chuckles*. That was just something I wasn't in to. I guess she didn't like me because she thought I was boojee; I wasn't loud and ignorant. I was really quiet and shy until you got to know me. I have always been observant when getting to know people so that's why at first when we meet I'm quiet it's because I'm listening and feeling you out. I would still keep a smile on my face so you wouldn't even know I'm checking you out but if you didn't take the time to get to know me you got the quiet and shy Sonya. Even then when I opened up to you I was never loud and ignorant, I was more of a silly person always trying to make you laugh. Since I'm always smiling. Now, I can laugh loud if you take me there so loud isn't always bad it's just when you throw ignorance into the equation. I love to smile so it was addictive but if I sensed you didn't like me of course I'm not going to be myself when you're around.

I was with him for 5years. Half of that time he spent locked up for selling drugs and robbing people. The first 2 and half years I did with him was the worst. All the stories you hear about people boarding a bus at the crack of dawn to ride 5 hours to a prison just to spend 2 or 3 hours with your loved one is ohh so real and to do that for 2 and a half years. I was loyal or a fool, whatever you want to call it. This was a burden I carried all these years my parents never knew what I was going thru with this guy.

I knew deep down inside that wasn't the life for me or my kids, believe me when they say love is blind it is, or maybe I was just settling. He promised everything from the sun to the moon and the stars that when he would come home he was going to get a job, go back to school we were going to move out the city and start over. He wasnt home a good month before he started running with those same friends and his brother. So from that point on he was in and out of jail. I told him I wasn't doing another bid with him.

The signs were always there that God had so much better for me but when you're young and in love you ignore the signs and believe you can change that person. If they really wanted to change, they would see how well you are doing without breaking the law or getting in trouble for it and it would motivate them to change. He didn't really want to change. You can't change anyone that doesn't want to change. It starts within them.

We tried to get married so many times but once again it apparently was not Gods will for my life. He was shot and killed right after New Year's Eve into New Year's day in the middle of the night leaving my son without a father. That devastated my son to the point that he would start acting out. He never had a male role model in his life. When his father was living he was too busy in the streets to take time out for him. What really devastated my son was the Christmas before the New Year when he was killed. He made a promise to my son that he was going to spend more time with him and not so much time in the streets.

My son never got the opportunity to experience that. It hurts me to my heart even today knowing the hurt he felt when we were told that his dad was killed. I believe my son's father felt something on that New Year's Eve, because he called me around 2 in the afternoon to wish me a Happy New Year in case he didn't see me or speak to me, which is what he said and to talk to his son. To top things off because his mother didn't like me she didn't accept my son who was innocent to it all.

We were banned from his funeral. She said if we showed up she would have security throw us out or because she was ghetto she would have people there to get at me (if you know what I mean, shaking my head), as if we killed her son. So needless to say my son didn't get to see his father for the last time. Even to this day they never had a relationship. We tried to make peace on several occasions so that burden wouldn't weigh on our hearts and cause bitterness but to no avail. She would go the lengths of seeing it's us at her door and wouldn't even open it to let us in, or when my son was older he would try to reach out to her and she would cuss him out over the phone.

But because we serve an awesome God we are free since we tried to reach out several times and make amends. You can't help who you fall in love with and I don't use that word lightly. I'm very picky and don't give of myself easily it's a process with me. I have always been a private person and I've always had a wall up. If you can make it past that wall then you are in there. From that point on I love hard so that's why my relationships lasted so long. I know we live in a microwave society where everything needs to be quick and easy and no one wants to work on anything, but I was never a quitter. I don't give up easy. Maybe that's why God had to remove some people out of my life so I could move on.

The only thing I regret for my son is he never had a male role model in his life so as a young child he would mimic my daughters. I would put him in basketball and all the after school programs just so he would have male influences but it didn't appear to work. I even tried all those mentor programs for boys and girls alike, they are not as easily accessible as you would think. I found out my daughter used to torture him, dress him up like a little girl so now he's fighting an identity spirit. He believes he was supposed to be a female who is trapped in a male's body. I minister to him and pray for him daily and I believe God for the victory. I struggled with that for a long time because of my beliefs. My son tried to hide it from me until he started feeling comfortable in his own skin and he turned 18.

I believe in loving people for whats in their heart but I just couldn't grasp the concept of him not wanting to be the little man that I raised. I have a lot of gay friends so it really didn't matter to me what their preference was. I would just pray and intercede on their behalf but when it hits home, that was a different kind of hurt. God delivered me from that hurt because we all have sinned and fallen short of Gods Glory. Once God speaks to your heart and you repent it's the same way he speaks to them and they can go before God for forgiveness

Romans 3:23For all have sinned, and come short of the glory of God

Time For A Change

Change represents uncertainty. With uncertainty comes insecurity and worry. The truth is that change isn't always a joyful, happy time, but rather a time to act like things are unfolding perfectly. That's what it seems to be for a lot of us: that stuff you have to plaster a smile over and pretend to embrace, even when your heart is drowning. Most of us want change as much as we are afraid of it. We say things like, I'm so unhappy in my marriage, but I'm afraid of being alone. I'm sick of working in corporate, but I have no idea what else I would do. I can't stand where I live, but my home is paid off.

When we resist change, it's because we're still holding on to what we know we need to release. Whether it's planned or unplanned change, we are being asked to re-examine our life and consider what direction really matters most. Change is part of life. And whether you like it or not, it's going to take place with or without your approval. It could be something pint-size (your favorite ice cream joint shut down), or gigantic (death, divorce, or disability). Life has a natural way of balancing things out. Based on my own experience change is much more enjoyable if you make a change instead of waiting for it to happen for you.

My father was a southern boy and every summer we would drive to Georgia to get away from the city and I enjoyed it. The people were so friendly and always smiling and waving. I remember the first time I came down I was sitting on the steps of a family members house and cars as they would drive by would honk their horns and wave and I would say to myself, I don't know you. That's when I found out that's just their mannerism. Everyone in New York was always so serious and always in a hurry. So there was no speaking or saying hi. By me being a New Yorker I never noticed that until I visited other states and saw the difference. Eventually, I decided to leave New York and move South It was definitely different from growing up in the City. My family had already moved years earlier but because I was trying to make it work with my son's father I kept making excuses as to why I didn't want to move. I really was tired of all the crime and stress of the city life. I felt so relaxed when I would come south. When I finally made up in my mind to make that move for myself and my children I realized it was Gods will all along because I started working within the first week and within a month I had my own space so life was good.

I really noticed the different type of men in Atlanta from what I was used to in New York. Atlanta has a lot of successful men and women doing their own thing, so I was definitely feeling Atlanta. The only thing I didn't't like was the women to men ratio here, like 10 women to 1 man. Some men would take that and run with it, because they believe they can get away with anything like being scrubs. In spite of the numbers though women still run the game. We have learned to ignore the lames and the scrubs. We workout, have great jobs, multiple degrees, high performing portfolios, rental properties, on-call hairdressers and personal chefs if need be.

Even with that being said though about the women to men ratio some successful women still tend to settle with the lames and the scrubs just so they won't be alone. I found myself dating on occasion but not really taking anyone seriously. In Atlanta you also get so much more for your money. If you sell your brownstone or house in New York let's say for example $400,000. You can come to Atlanta buy some land, build a 5 bedroom 4 bathroom house with a huge back yard, pool, swings and slides on the other end of the yard and still have a couple hundred thousand left over. You can't beat that. That's Just a scenario numbers may not be completely accurate but very close. That's why so many northerners come south for a better way of living.

After years of providing for my family independently and being successful at it. Taking vacations with the kids every year, it was getting lonely. There was still that void I felt. Like something was missing I always said when I got married I was only going to get married once. I don't take it lightly that's why I took my time trying to weed out the jokers. Needless to say I didn't do a good job.

So eventually I did get married to a southern boy who won my heart over. He was very good at fronting and perpetrating. He made it appear as though he had it all together. I wasn't looking for this big time producer or basketball player; I was just looking for someone who was a hard worker, honest and loyal. I don't know why he felt the need to try and impress me. Eventually, the truth will come out so why even go thru all that trouble. He claimed to have found his Queen. He portrayed himself as a good provider. That was ok since I was already able to provide for me and my family, that was a plus. He was a God fearing man and had big dreams and aspirations so what more could a girl ask for, right? I know the only perfect being was Jesus Christ. We all fall short and have things we go to God for deliverance from. So, I ignored the signs. He would always throw up all the businesses he created in his name but none were profitable, they were more of a tax liability.

Now by this time when I got married I was saved going to church every chance I could and had a better understanding of the Bible. I knew about being submissive to your husband and following him as he follows Christ. I was able to do that but had to learn how to change my form of thinking from I to us and to not be so independent. It was hard not being in control all the time but after 7 years I got good at it. I was still a hard worker and always tried to maintain the Spirit of Excellence, so certain things I wouldn't compromise on.

Why is it so important to develop a spirit of excellence? Why is it that God speaks to us about such a spirit? Each of us will be faced with "tests" of one sort or another throughout our lives. We need to realize, for example, that what makes a good marriage is not how infatuated we are with each other but how well we can come through the tests. The spirit with which we face these "tests" will tell us a great deal about its outcome. And, you can tell a great deal about someone by observing the results of their tests.

Daniel possessed specific qualities in such abundance that it was credited to him as having a spirit of excellence. These qualities included the following; extraordinary spirit is known by others as having a positive attitude, always bringing a fresh perspective to each problem and it gives others hope. Knowledge and Insight is known as a person who constantly increasing in knowledge and as one who gives wise counsel that always brings understanding.

Interpretation of dreams is described as a person that, whatever circumstances arise, I can always discern what God is saying. As I share God's perspective, it brings confidence and direction to others.

Explanation of enigmas is having a reputation of making difficult issues simple and comprehendible. Solving difficult problems is known as one that others look to when complicated issues arise. I am able to solve these in such a way that everyone benefits and each person feels valued.

When we possess the spirit of excellence, God guards us and enables us to actually influence the nation. We have that same potential to become a people with a spirit of excellence. So the Bible shows us with Daniel's life what it means to have a spirit of excellence.

"Therefore, putting aside all malice and all deceit and hypocrisy and envy and all slander, like newborn babies, long for pure milk of the word, so you may grow in respect to salvation"**1Peter. 2:1-2.** In other words, once and for all put aside all these things and thus begin to develop a spirit of excellence.

Daniel simply did not engage in anything unless it was honest. It was his basis for life, his "default" setting. A lot of times we know that something is the right choice, but we've got to reach towards it; we struggle for it. The question is who are we when no one is looking? At the very core of his being, Daniel possessed a genuine character. So how can we get to that point where our choices are automatic and we don't have to struggle for it? Well, Daniel reached that level because; Daniel learned to "feed" himself on the words of the Lord even while he was young. He was able to stand on his own spiritually. That's why it's so important to have our own devotional or quiet times so we learn to hear from God ourselves. We need to wean off of blaming others for our circumstances. Like Daniel we must learn to stand on our own and make wise decisions. Another way we can develop genuine character is by learning from Daniel:

Here's the toughest thing about developing the spirit of excellence. There will be seasons in our lives when following God won't be easy. God will tell us to change our attitudes, to be gracious, generous, polite, or to protect rather than taking advantage of —and it's going to be tough. But, "...those who are mature...have trained themselves to recognize the difference between right and wrong and then do what is right" **Hebrews. 5:14.**
So there will be times we'll feel like hypocrites in our practice of certain qualities because we are stretching to reach that point. Yet regardless of how we feel, we must

be obedient and do what we know is right. The key is to keep training until it becomes genuine. Soon we develop a trained, disciplined heart. And as we develop that kind of character, the next point we learn from David is that… "Take your everyday ordinary life – your sleeping, eating, going-to-work life – and place it before God as an offering…Don't become so well-adjusted to your culture that you fit into it without even thinking. Instead, fix your attention on God. You'll be changed from the inside out" **Romans. 12:2.**

When you get up in the morning, try to get to your knees before you get to your feet so that you can pray. Pray something like this: "Heavenly Father, You didn't have to get me up this morning, or give me another breath but You did. And because You did, I know that my assignment on earth isn't done yet. Therefore, help me to love You with all my heart, soul, mind and strength. And, Lord, would You help me to please You with the thoughts I think". If you please God with your thoughts, your actions will easily follow. On the other hand, if our thoughts are not right, we will never mature even if we do the right things. That's why God wants to change us from the inside out and to do that we must fix our attention on God. So though we may sometimes feel uncomfortable doing what is right, we need to practice until it becomes comfortable. That way our default system changes, we operate out of a genuine character, and thus comfortable with our faith.

Please be aware that even though we may have changed our ways, bad things can still keep surfacing. That's because the seed sown from our past actions are reaping bad fruit. This is the point where most people bail out. Nevertheless, we need to stay true during this season and not give up because the third step in developing a "spirit of excellence" is to realize that…God notices when we develop a spirit of excellence. In any situation, God can predict a favorable outcome because He watches how we deal with problems in our lives. That's why it's important that we, "Consider yourselves fortunate when all kinds of trials come your way, for you know that when your faith succeeds in facing such trials, the result is the ability to endure…so that you may be perfect and complete, lacking nothing" **James 1:2-4** .

Whenever Daniel solved a problem, a miracle followed. How do miracles happen in our lives? Well God is looking for people with a spirit of excellence. If people can predict how well you will fare in a problem, it gives them assurance for the future. Like Daniel, we too can develop a spirit of excellence. We can be known for our genuine character because we know the difference between right and wrong and choose to do what is right. People will be assured that regardless of our lack of experience or knowledge, we will be able to handle things because we are comfortable with our faith and therefore demonstrate the measure of our faith. I think this world could use a lot more "Daniels". You have the potential. Let's ask God to help us develop that spirit of excellence!

So, outside of having the Spirit of Excellence, or striving for it at least, my bills were paid. I was still able to buy the nice things I wanted as long as I was working and able. I introduced him to the finer things in life, which was a first for me because I was always surrounded by the people that already had them. I was trying something different. They say if you want different results you have to try something different.

There were times in my marriage where I felt like the man in the relationship as far as being the provider and keeping a roof over our heads. Even though we were supposed to have been as one unit I always felt I was doing more to maintain the household and his money went towards his dreams and aspirations. Example: when you spend your whole check on expensive equipment for your dream job but your dream job is not putting money in your pocket, it just looks good on paper. Thus, not allowing me to follow mine. When I complained I was the one called selfish and not being supportive when all I really wanted was some help.

Selfishness; characterized by or manifesting concern or care only for oneself and Stubbornness; fixed or set in purpose or opinion are different from independence. Losing your identity is not a prerequisite for a successful marriage. Selfishness (Me focused behavior) and Stubbornness (a resistance or unwillingness to change or modify destructive behaviors) are definitely on the list of No-No's for marriage. Humility to Gods will is a good thing but blindly becoming a doormat like (do whatever you want honey you're the man and I won't say boo!) Is not independence being laid down nor is it smart.

I believe your home takes precedence over everything.

You can't put all your money into your dreams and let your household suffer. You should be able to take care of home and put money aside to go towards your dreams. What good is investing in your dreams and your family is in the dark or they don't have a roof over their heads. So, you move the family into your business and give up the house. Something is seriously wrong with that picture. Now here's the kicker. At one point I was no longer working so I had to solely depend on him and that was the worst mistake of my life. My personal Bills were put on the back burner. My independence was gone and slowly but surely so was my self-esteem. I fell into a deep depression. All I kept remembering was what my Dad used to say about not depending on a man to take care of you, you should always have some money saved, so I was confused

Now, my dad didn't go to church so I can understand how he didn't have the concept of marriage correct and how the Bible says a man that finds a wife finds a good thing. She is to follow him as he follows Christ. Being humble and allowing him to lead, making me dependent on a man. My Ex was an Elder in the church that his best friend was a Pastor of. We were always in church, which I loved so I just knew I was being obedient. I let a lot of things slide. He decided to let his best friend counsel us when we were having issues, which was a disaster because it was one sided. He would make comments to my ex like man you are good because I would have left and stuff like that so I was bamboozled.

Instead of being neutral and understanding there are two sides to every relationship and there's also something called; Cause and effect; which in a relationship between events or things, where one is the result of the other or others. This is a combination of action and reaction. So the whole session turned out to be Sonya this is what you need to do and change to make your marriage work. I of course didn't agree but I was not being heard. My opinions didn't matter because he was this awesome man of God. That same Pastor later on left his wife of twenty something years, 7 kids later and re married. I told my ex we needed someone neutral who didn't know us personally. He didn't think so because he was pleased with what the Pastor was saying. What I didn't do was pray. He had a very jealous, selfish and manipulative spirit He could convince you that the sky was purple even though you know the color of the sky and you see it with your own eyes he had a way with words.

Perfect Example: True story. We were visiting my family in Atlanta for Thanksgiving. We came a day early because I had some business to take care of before the holiday and he knew this. So, we are here in Atlanta. I asked him if he wanted to come and run around with me. He said he would stay back at my family member's house to relax. They told him to help himself to anything he wanted in the refrigerator while we were gone. So it took me some hours to do what I had to do which was beyond my control.

When I got back to the house to my surprise he was all upset, he had called all of his family back home and told them I left him to die with no food (his words not mine). It wasn't his house so he wasn't going in the fridge. He was diabetic so he says he didn't eat all day but before I left he was ok with getting the food out the fridge. So, because his family didn't know the whole story they believed him. Despite the fact that he was over dramatic I was painted as this villain, this horrible person. If he felt some type of way with me being gone he should have said that. He didn't call me to say he needed anything. I just came back to that. Needless to say after that he was ready to leave when he should have just come with me in the first place or as a grown man get in the kitchen and heat him up something to eat.

I believe satan used him to try and break me down to nothing. I was too confident. He was enjoying the control he had over my life. He moved me to another state leaving behind all my friends and family. So I didn't have any support system. He didn't want me to have friends outside of him. He was good for telling me things like I don't know why you like them they are the same ones that's always talking bad about you. We were always surrounded by his friends, so whenever there was an issue between us they would treat me differently so I know he talked about our business outside of me, him and God and I was miserable. While, he was portrayed as this wonderful, loving, God fearing man, that I was lucky to have. The devil is a liar!! When you can't own up to your own imperfections and you honestly believe everything is someone else's fault, that's an issue. It takes two people to destroy a marriage, not just one. It's called Ownership. Own up to your faults.

I was worst off financially and mentally married than I was single and independent. Something was wrong with that picture All I kept thinking was I can do badly all by myself. So the enemy had me fooled. I played my part also since I was unhappy and you knew I was unhappy that's a true saying *Happy Wife, Happy life* I would do tit for tat which only made it worst. His mistake was thinking that he could take care of me when he really couldn't and it became overwhelming to him. He could barely take care of himself. No matter how hard it got I tried to stick it out, but eventually I had to free myself from that bondage for my sanity and pray for God's forgiveness. I honestly felt God frowned on Divorce and I would be punished for leaving. I went into a deep deep depression though for about 2 years. God allowed me to become broken before him so that I could hear him. I wasn't happy in it and I wasn't happy out of it. I didn't want to be bothered with anyone. I would isolate myself from family and friends I had to start all over. It truly felt like a death and it was, it was the death of a relationship that was vowed before God that you would be in until death do us part.

Depression

Too many people take marriage lightly as if it's just the dating game with a piece of paper. I never in my life felt that kind of pain. God had to get me to a place where he could really get my attention and minister to me. I was broken. I wasn't going to church anymore which was a big mistake. Depression affects people because they get so wrapped up with the process of living day to day that they begin to lose interest in their life and what they are going thru so they neglect God's word. They feel the weight of serving God because the joy is gone and they are left with the dull mechanics of living. Like a dark tunnel with no exit

King Saul was affected by depression. He called for David to play and sing the anointed Psalms. Of all cities in the world, none has been so frequently attacked like Jerusalem. Why is it so? It is because the place has a prophetic destiny. So, as a child of God, in case you are seriously under attack or you are wondering why you are sweating and struggling, it means that there is something in your destiny that the enemy does not want to happen:

Isaiah 59:19
So shall they fear the name of the LORD from the west, and his glory from the rising of the sun. When the enemy shall come in like a flood, the Spirit of the LORD shall lift up a standard against him.

You can give in to depression or resist it. When you offer yourselves to someone/something as obedient slaves, you are slaves of the one you obey—whether you are slaves to sin, which leads to death, or to obedience, which leads to righteousness:

Romans 6:16

Know ye not, that to whom ye yield yourselves servants to obey, his servants ye are to whom ye obey; whether of sin unto death, or of obedience unto righteousness?

Don't give in to the spirit of heaviness – but use the word of God like a sword. When the devil says your no good remind him of:

2 Corinthians 5:17 Therefore if any man be in Christ, he is a new creature: old things are passed away; behold, all things are become new.

When the devil says you're not saved just tell him I know I'm saved because I was there when it happened. When the devil says to worry, just remind him that God said don't worry about anything. When the devil says be sick just tell him by his stripes I am healed. When he says be afraid remind him God said my peace I give to you. When he says be defeated you say we are more than conquerors through him that loved us.

We are all going to face adversity. Even Paul did. A person comes under attack because the enemy wants to conquer him, the enemy wants to suppress him, the enemy wants to contend with his destiny, his existence is threatening the existence of another person or his destiny is an eagle destiny.

2 Corinthians 1:3-11

Blessed be the God and Father of our Lord Jesus Christ, the Father of mercies and God of all comfort, who comforts us in all our tribulation, that we may be able to comfort those who are in any trouble, with the comfort with which we ourselves are comforted by God. For as the sufferings of Christ abound in us, so our consolation also abounds through Christ. Now if we are afflicted, it is for your consolation and salvation, which is effective for enduring the same sufferings which we also suffer. Or if we are comforted, it is for your consolation and salvation. And our hope for you is steadfast, because we know that as you are partakers of the sufferings, so also you will partake of the consolation. For we do not want you to be ignorant, brethren, of our trouble which came to us in Asia: that we were burdened beyond measure, above strength, so that we despaired even of life. Yes, we had the sentence of death in ourselves, that we should not trust in ourselves but in God who raises the dead, who delivered us from so great a death, and does deliver us; in whom we trust that He will still deliver us, you also helping together in prayer for us, that thanks may be given by many persons on our behalf for the gift granted to us through many.

How to Bind the enemy: Satan, in the name of Jesus, I bind your spirit of heaviness. I recognize that you have taken advantage of me. Now I resist you in Jesus name Amen.

James 4:7 says "Resist the devil and he will flee from you." Go in the name of Jesus and don't bother coming back again.

Matthew 18:18
Verily I say unto you, Whatsoever ye shall bind on earth shall be bound in heaven: and whatsoever ye shall loose on earth shall be loosed in heaven.
Don't you know that when you offer yourselves to someone as obedient slaves, you are slaves of the one you obey—whether you are slaves to sin, which leads to death, or to obedience, which leads to righteousness How to Loose – Holy Ghost, oil of joy, praise. Praise silences the devil. **1John 4:4**. Jesus also said, "ALL POWER is given unto ME in Heaven and in Earth!"-- **Matthew 28:18**--And YOU have JESUS and all of HIS power! He says, "Behold, I give unto you POWER over ALL the power of the Devil**!"--Luke 10:19**. So through the power of prayer in JESUS' NAME you can rebuke the Enemy & order him to "go jump in the lake and get the Heck out of here!" when he tries to oppress or distress you by speaking to your mind and tempting you with negative or discouraging thoughts!--And he HAS to obey you and FLEE**!--James 4:7**.

Psalms 8:1-2
O LORD our Lord, how excellent is thy name in all the earth! who hast set thy glory above the heavens. Out of the mouth of babes and sucklings hast thou ordained strength because of thine enemies, that thou mightest still the enemy and the avenger.

That you might still – that you make the devil shut up!

In Matthew, Jesus said thou hast perfected praise – he was interpreting the scripture not misquoting. Praise is a garment of the spirit. Put on the garment of praise for the spirit of heaviness. We must literally cloth ourselves in praise. We must put it on. Every morning we decide what to wear. In the same way we must decide to put on the garment of praise. In Hebrews the word used for garment was more than something draped around the shoulders but it literally teaches us to wrap or cover ourselves in praise. The garment of praise is to leave no openings or holes which hostile spirits can penetrate. When you are – then put on praise. Praise prepares us for miracles. Something in Jonah's prayer got the attention of God – praise.

Jonah 2:9-10
But I will sacrifice unto thee with the voice of thanksgiving; I will pay that that I have vowed. Salvation is of the LORD.
And the LORD spake unto the fish, and it vomited out Jonah upon the dry land.

Paul and Silas. **Acts 16:16-21**

Once when we were going to the place of prayer, we were met by a female slave who had a spirit by which she predicted the future. She earned a great deal of money for her owners by fortune-telling. 17 She followed Paul and the rest of us, shouting, "These men are servants of the Most High God, who are telling you the way to be saved." 18 She kept this up for many days. Finally Paul became so annoyed that he turned around and said to the spirit, "In the name of

Jesus Christ I command you to come out of her!" At that moment the spirit left her.

When her owners realized that their hope of making money was gone, they seized Paul and Silas and dragged them into the marketplace to face the authorities. They brought them before the magistrates and said, "These men are Jews, and are throwing our city into an uproar by advocating customs unlawful for us Romans to accept or practice.

Acts 16:25
And at midnight Paul and Silas prayed, and sang praises unto God: and the prisoners heard them.

Put on the garments of Praise. Hebrew word – tehillah – to sing praise. It is used in **Psalm 22:3** where it says God inhabits the praise of his people. God manifest himself in the midst of exuberant singing. God sent ambushments; those who attack suddenly and unexpectedly from a concealed position.

2 Chronicles. 20:22
Now when they began to sing and to praise

Psalm 34:1 I will bless the Lord at all times his PRAISE shall continually be in my mouth.

Psalm 40:1-3
I waited patiently for the Lord ; And He inclined to me, And heard my cry. He also brought me up out of a horrible pit, Out of the miry clay, And set my feet

upon a rock, And established my steps. He has put a new song in my mouth— Praise to our God; Many will see it and fear, And will trust in the Lord.

Psalm 66:1-2
Make a joyful shout to God, all the earth! Sing out the honor of His name; Make His praise glorious.

God is surrounded in a city, by a wall called salvation. The way to get into that city is through the gate of praise. We don't gain access to his presence by needs and petitions but by praise. I didn't know that at the time I just felt I needed time to be by myself and heal. Guys would come after me hard, like they were thirsty. It was almost like satan told them to pursue me hard at my most vulnerable point but I just wasn't interested. I was into something much deeper than that. I was trying to find myself again and get my independence back because I was happiest when I could do for myself and not having to depend on anyone to do anything for me but God.

Now, is it just me or does it look like from my experiences, I can't speak for anyone else's that if you want to be successful you have to be independent in order to maintain your own level of success? The moment you put your success in someone else's hands they no longer value you as being that strong and independent person you were when they met you. You become a possession that can be controlled. Don't get me wrong I'm all for marriage and building an empire where you both are successful. Does it take a special kind of person that will not get the big head knowing they have that much power over another human being that used to be so powerful to them? Does it make them feel accomplished like a conqueror?

Men enjoy independence. A man's sense of self-worth is determined when he "feels" in-charge. When God made man, He gave him a task (taking care of the garden). He feels better about himself when he is free to do things and handle problems on his own. This is why men are often resistant to their spouse trying to change them. The more the wife tries to "improve" him, the more he tries to resist her. It makes the man feel like his partner doesn't trust his ability to deal with life. He resists her input and she persists in trying to be a helper by making him the "target."

In my opinion and I'm only going off my experiences some men are attracted to independent women just as long as they don't out shine them or make more money than they do because then it messes with their self-esteem. Men like to feel needed and wanted even if you feel you don't need them. If they don't have that reassurance that they still are the man in the relationship their egos meaning self-esteem or self-image; feelings: get in the way. I hope I'm helping someone.

Why Does It Still Hurt?

For a longtime, I really did think I was being punished by God but my Spiritual Mother who I love dearly (Another strong independent woman). She took the time to minister to me and helped me understand that I was going thru a transition. My Spirit was awakened by her teachings and I began to get that hunger and thirst again for the Word. I can't explain the feeling but my Spirit was and is hooked to the knowledge, wisdom and understanding that I am now receiving from the Word being taught to me by this mighty woman of God. I just want her to know what a huge impact she made on my life, I was listening. Your teachings were not in vain. I want you to know that and I want to make you proud.

She is definitely a gift from God. He led me to her at the weakest point in my life to let me know I still have a purpose that was already ordained by God and if I'm ready to listen and adhere to what thus sayeth the Lord! My Life will never be the same. God knows exactly who and what you need to get your attention.

Romans 10:13-15
For whosoever shall call upon the name of the Lord shall be saved.
How then shall they call on him in whom they have not believed? and how shall they believe in him of whom they have not heard? and how shall they hear without a preacher?
And how shall they preach, except they be sent? as it is written, How beautiful are the feet of them that

preach the gospel of peace, and bring glad tidings of good things!

I really didn't understand all the feelings I was having and why my desire was so strong for the Holy Spirit. The Love and respect I have for this woman of God was like no other and I couldn't explain it. I stopped trying to question God and get an understanding and just let the Lord speak to me and show me the things in me that were not of him. The things I needed to change. I found my answers in the Word. I understand now what the Agape love is Agape (Ancient Greek ἀγάπη, agápē) is a Greco-Christian term referring to "love: the highest form of love, charity", and "the love of God for man and of man for God".

God was molding me and reshaping me to get me back on the right track towards my destiny since the enemy pulled me off course. My transition was not personal it was my testimony so I would be able to help someone else, while giving God the Glory for overcoming it. God gives us the freedom of choice and sometimes we get deceived and choose the other path that God has not chosen for us, so he will allow us to go down that path and when we hit that barrier in the road he waits for us to cry out to him before he takes control again.

So, why does it still hurt? God showed me my heart and all the scrapes and bruises that were still there. All the pain from past relationships, feeling like an outcast in your own family and the rejections I received mainly from women because they never took the time to really know me before judging me. Why am I constantly being misjudged by my outer appearance and not my heart? All pretty girls are not shallow, selfish and boojee. I say that with confidence meaning belief in oneself and one's powers or abilities; self-confidence; self-reliance; assurance not conceit meaning an excessively favorable opinion of one's own ability, importance, wit, etc. because I had to learn to love me and stop looking for someone to love me and fill that void. Have you ever felt like the black sheep of your family? A term used to describe someone who feels left out in a family. Basically, the outcast of the family because they choose to do other things or someone who is treated different than the rest. No matter what good you try to do, evil was always present turning that good deed or good thing into something the total opposite of what you were trying to do. So those who don't really know your heart or refuse to see your heart will continue to think bad about you.

Have you always felt rejected when you would show love and never got it back in return the way you would have liked or so it seemed? Something you may have experienced your entire life and continue to experience it today by men/women you've loved who want nothing to do with you for some reason. Those who have never experienced it cannot know the pain and emotional damage it causes. It makes you feel depressed, lonely and like a worthless reject who will never amount to anything or find someone worthy to love or love you in return for who you are because you are not good enough. It's the worst and loneliest feeling a person could ever experience.

The people closest to you. would be the main ones always seeing the negative in you and never seeing the positive? It would get so bad that you are afraid to show love for fear of rejection. You try to dance around it in person but are able express it on paper. So if you do get rejected from something you have written its nowhere near the pain of being rejected in person. It's harder for some people to open up emotionally to someone in person because they feel it is a sign of weakness so they would rather be cautious just to protect the heart. Well you're not alone. God has a special purpose on your life. The enemy knows this so anything he can do to draw you further and further away from your destiny he will do it. Even if it means stealing your joy, self-esteem and self-worth.

We have to understand that it's not the people that are coming against us it's the Spirit that's being used for that assignment, so praying and rebuking is the only way to get them to flee from you. Responding in the Carnal mind, meaning physically and emotionally will only add fuel to the fire. So why does it still hurt? It still hurts as a reminder to take that pain and convert it into something positive. It's also a reminder of where God has bought you from. Your purpose is in your pain.

We all experience pain in life. Heartache, loss, disappointment. Suffering is a part of being human. When you're in the depths of it, it can be hard to see how you can ever recover from your deep pain. The idea that you might one day be grateful for your disappointment and hurt seems unthinkable. Yet, we always have a choice. Even in our pain we have a choice to make. We get to decide whether we will take the opportunity and grow, or whether we will let it consume us.

I by no means intend to make this seem simple; it may be the hardest thing you will ever do. But your pain may also be the thing that pushes you towards your greatest personal breakthroughs. It is our hurt that can crack us open and let the light in. It is our pain that can help move us towards living a more deeply fulfilling life. There is a psychological idea known as Post-Traumatic Growth. We are all familiar with its cousin, post-traumatic stress. Post-traumatic growth isn't discussed as frequently, but it is the concept that explains how many of us take our pain and use it as the energy to grow psychologically.

Post-traumatic growth is not about returning to the same life as it was previously experienced before a period of traumatic suffering; but rather it is about undergoing significant 'life-changing' psychological shifts in thinking and relating to the world, that contribute to a personal process of change, that is deeply meaningful. We need to get in touch with our emotions, and be willing to feel them. To understand why we hurt, we have to dip deep into where the pain is stemming from. It is easy to say we are hurt because of heartbreak, but the question is, what part of the heartbreak is really causing us the pain? Is it that we feel like a failure? That we are grieving for a future that no longer exists? Or that we don't feel worthy of love? We need to express our emotions and work through them until we can find their root cause. Self-reflection and personal understanding is a prerequisite to deeper psychological growth. In order to grow from a painful experience, we need to focus our minds on looking for the lesson. This is one way of choosing to have a growth-mindset. No matter what the situation, we will be able to uncover a lesson if we look hard enough. If you have been faced with an illness, perhaps it can teach you what you need to prioritize in life. If you are recovering from heartbreak, perhaps it can highlight your need to respect yourself more, so that you are not prone to letting other people disrespect you.

Looking for the lesson is about taking your power back. You can't wallow indefinitely in the pain if you are to step up and grow. Once you've identified the root cause of your hurt, you have the power to look for what you can learn from the situation. Once you can acknowledge what your current situation might have to teach you, you need to resolve to change. Real positive growth must be followed by action. You have to do things differently. This is where your pain can truly turn into your greatest power.

It may be that you re-prioritize how you live your life, so that the things that really matter to you play a bigger part. Or you may try to focus on truly deep-down loving yourself before you begin to look for another romantic partner. Your actions will always be so personal to you. Real growth comes from a willingness to change. You need to do things differently and use your pain as the thing that leads you on your path to growth. You can turn your pain into power. If you are willing to work out where the pain stems from, recognize there is a lesson to be learned, and turn your new knowledge into action, you will come through the suffering a brighter and stronger person. I hope I'm helping someone.

Transitioning

Now, when my transition started, meaning when I decided to leave my marriage. I was homeless because I was in another state away from my family; I was staying in a hotel that was becoming costly. I didn't have the means at that time to move back home yet. Transitioning can be very painful, but in the long run it's worth it to just be true to yourself. If it wasn't for my Godmother who opened up her heart and her home for me while I was going thru, I don't know where I would be right now. She was really my Ex's God Mother but when we met our spirits just clicked. I thank God for her every day. She was truly a blessing when no one else was around.

She of course was a strong independent woman at the time maintaining her own career and her 5 bedroom, 4 bathroom house. So, needless to say I had everything I needed in front of me to inspire me to get back on my feet. I lost everything my furniture was in storage about to be auctioned off because it wasn't getting paid. My truck started breaking down on me, one thing after the other kept going wrong with it and with no money to fix it I couldn't drive it.

Everything that could have gone wrong went wrong and because he defamed my name: meaning to attack the good name or reputation of, as by uttering or publishing maliciously or falsely anything injurious; slander or libel; calumniate to his family and friends that didn't really know me, making himself the victim, I had no love or support. I was in a strange state and I felt completely alone. She opened up her home for me giving me my own room with my own bathroom until I got myself together and was able to move back home to my family, where my sister stepped in until I branched back out on my own. It took me getting my independence back to get my Joy back, my self-esteem and my self-worth, my heart opened up again and I was receptive to others. I found myself in a very happy place where I was able to really show love to people in spite of what they showed me. I no longer had that wall up. Thank you Jesus! I forgive him for everything he did to me and I thank him at the same time because now I know my true destiny and I am not blinded by the enemies' tricks and deceit. I would not have been able to find peace, joy and happiness if I didn't forgive.

Which would have still given him power over me and my destiny. So, Thank you Jesus for clarity. I could no longer keep this all bottled up inside. This is my testimony with hopes I'm helping someone else who maybe going thru the same situation or something very similar. Never allow people to break you down and dictate what type of person you are. If they have nothing positive to say, ever about you. Then you need to separate yourself from them because they mean you no good.

Negativity is characterized by the absence of distinguishing or marked qualities or features; lacking positive attributes a dull, lifeless, negative character lacking in constructiveness, helpfulness, optimism, or cooperativeness. If you hear it enough you may start to believe the lies, which will affect your self-esteem and self-worth. The word love is an action word; too many people use that word loosely and cant back it up with their actions. Let the love they proclaim to have for you show thru their actions which comes from the heart which is the center of the total personality, especially with reference to intuition, feelings, or emotions. If it's truly from their heart it will stay consistent and will be unconditional. You can't fake it too long, eventually your true heart will be revealed. Out of respect and not wanting to make anyone look bad I withheld names because someone needs to hear this.

A woman is beautiful because of the way she thinks. She is beautiful because of the way she shows love. She is beautiful because of the sparkle in her eyes. She is beautiful because she is a woman. Embrace how beautiful you are!!

I don't think being independent is a curse because as you can see even after all that I have gone thru. My ability to pull myself back up was due to my faith in God and my determination and drive to succeed at whatever it is I try to do. That came from what I was taught as a child independency. I believe the right person will nurture your independence and add to it instead of taking from it.

Independent doesn't mean that you are distant. Some People who see themselves as independent often use that to cover up stubbornness, selfishness and their fear of intimacy. So if anyone says they can't make time for you because they are "Independent" Cut them loose. Truly independent people know that they still have to give of themselves, emotionally open partners that are willing to compromise on important issues and to make time for those they love. Their independence is manifested in ways that ultimately promote intimacy and the long term health of their relationships by preventing the emotional burnout that many couples experience. In most relationships we can all be a little clingy. Men and women the same. From birth women and men are indoctrinated with the stereotype that women are uptight and insecure. When in fact Men are just as clingy.

There are plenty of relationships out there where both parties attach desperately to each other like saran wrap. The need to be together all the time. The need to constantly seek attention and love arises from a sense of insecurity, in oneself and in one's ability to hold on to a significant other in the viability of the relationship itself. However there are some people out there Men and women the same who are naturally independent and who bring that quality to bear on their love lives.

Some Independent people love having time to themselves, for many it's absolutely necessary. Whether it's having time alone at home, going to the movies by themselves or eating solo at a restaurant. The desire for solitude doesn't go away when you get into a relationship, instead we learn to balance the time spent with your significant others with much valued time apart.

This time away from each other can be vital in keeping the relationship fresh without burning out on each other. Some maintain separate social lives. They have their own friends and go to their own social events in addition to sharing some of them with one another. Maintaining an independent social life is good for any relationship because it's simply too much to expect each other to be able to fulfill all your social needs. If you get to have fun hanging out with friends, you put less pressure on each other to be your everything.

Some couples like checking in with each other many times throughout the day via email, texts and lunch hour phone calls. But for independent people, this kind of constant exchange feels unnecessary and irritating. Don't get me wrong I'm all for the desire to want to be able to interact with your loved one throughout the day to see how their day is going, but twice a day seems feasible. That way you can eliminate small talk and be able to talk about your day when you see each other.

We also understand by being independent that our loved ones need time away and need to have their separate identities. This can help the overall health of the relationship by allowing both people to maintain clear senses of self without any one becoming jealous or feeling insecure about the other. Being able to comfortably spend time apart is also an indication that you are secure in your relationship and not worrying about what the other person is doing, thinking or feeling. We have a very strong sense of who we are and what we want. When you really know yourself, you feel comfortable speaking up about what your desires and limits are. For some people, being in love means moving in as quickly as possible, where others are happy maintaining their separate living spaces for a while. Having their own space just means that they can continue to have valuable alone time when needed. When we finally do decide to move in together we do so after a lot of thoughtful consideration of how it will work so it will be a success. This is only from my past experiences of being so quick to live together without really thinking things thru.

One of the great rites of passage that isn't always defined as a rite is the acquisition of our independence. You're all grown up now so you can be taken seriously. We view the status of being independent as having made it or being accomplished as something to aspire to. I believe part of the reason we see it that way is because the option of being codependent doesn't seem to be a healthy thing in our minds.

We don't want to have to rely on anyone else for anything or to have a need from anyone else for anything because it is seen to be a sign of weakness. I think it's great that we learn to stand on our own two feet. When you are a child that's what you start out literally doing trying to get to find your footing. As you get older you're trying to find you're footing in other areas, like friendships, education and dressing yourself. As we progress we should be able to take care of the things that others used to do for us. Paying your own bills, fending for yourself and making your own decisions. When we talk about our independence we usually are referring to how good it is were able to take care of our own needs. For some of us, independence means being able to make our own significant financial moves such as buying your own car or your own house without the assistance of others.

Independence means being strong enough in our own career and purpose that we know we'll always somewhat be well equipped for the challenges in life. The interesting thing about independence or an attitude of independence is that it's usually born out of necessity. In many cases there are areas of your life where no one else has been there to look after you or maybe you've had to be the emotionally strong one because there hasn't been anyone else to do it for you. As a result when we have an attitude of independence it usually means we're not good at asking for help when we need it. Because in all previous experiences we've just risen above it and learned to make do.

No one else was going to be there for us, or maybe that's how we felt, so why should we belittle ourselves to seek anyone's help now? Maybe we don't think anyone would ever be there for us and we can have bitterness or anger towards needing the help of others. The truth is though that often we do need others to help us out. There are some challenges that are too big for just us, but because of our independence or spirit of pride in this case we refuse to let anyone help us. What I like about this attitude is that you take responsibility for your own well-being. More than just physical things you're usually pretty dedicated towards working through things and not letting things keep you down. It's a sense of ownership over your own life and it's a good thing when people take responsibility for how they are feeling and really owning their decisions.

You also probably aren't aware of or accommodating of your weaknesses. If you're so used to doing things your own way you're probably not aware that sometimes your own way isn't actually the right way. Example: You have a certain approach to your finances but your actually not aware of how bad you are at saving, you have an attitude towards the friends you make but you haven't invited in any other voices to give you the real truth about how you treat other people.

When you're used to playing for one it doesn't matter as much but if you want to grow and learn to be a team player in any area in your life you're going to need to invite the right feedback in to your life and not be so set on your way of doing things. With this you're able to look out for others too when you have the right balance of independence

You're on top of your own issues; you're more free to look after others. If our independence is complete isolation then we probably won't get this far cause were too obsessed with our own needs and priorities. But if we use it in the right way we can be ensured our lives are being taken care of and also we are able to extend to others.

Everything for yourself is that you only have resources and investments limited to one person to accomplish things. Its great you have enough for you and perhaps enough for others but if you're only ever living it out in an independent fashion your reach will only be as far as your reach can go. People say that if you want something done right do it yourself. Have you ever thought of it like this?   If you want something done right don't do it yourself? Involve others, if it's all about you then what happens when you're not able to be there?

If it's just your independent self-there's a good chance that you're not going to be able to make a lasting impression. There's such great power in partnership. So often we view it as tying ourselves down letting ourselves become codependent or that other people are getting in our way. Maybe that just shows us a real flaw in our attitude in that we don't actually know how to do things with others. When you have been independent so long it can be hard to change your mind set to incorporate others. But if we really want to be world changers were not going to be able to do it alone. We weren't't made to do it alone. Our destiny involves people, it doesn't shut them out. Of course there will be times where we are sent on by ourselves to face something's alone to build our character, but we need to remember that were not made to do our whole life alone and that our greatest strength lies in partnering with others and doing it as a team. With Independence also comes Self Confidence, its empowering to have the physical, emotional, mental capability to look after yourself, taking on challenges you would otherwise pass up. Financial Freedom. Possessing a few fixit and maintenance skills is liberating and cost effective recognizing signs of trouble. It allows you to take action before irreversible damage occurs because calling a tradesperson or mechanic every time can cost time and money.

Freedom that you can take on the world and do anything you can but Freedom needs to be exercised wisely. Convenience is often a lot quicker, less expensive and less frustrating to be able to correct a problem rather than having to wait for help or someone's approval. Resilience in knowing stuff happens to everyone, but when you know you can sort something out even if it's a mess or may take a while you will bounce back from adversity more quickly. Resourcefulness, when you're on your own and things go wrong there's no one around besides you to figure things out. Sure you can call for help but learning how to get out of a predicament teaches us a lot more about what we are capable of and all we can accomplish when help isn't available. Also, again with independence it is very hard to ask for help. It can feel demeaning. Most of us would much sooner offer help than receive it because we know how fulfilling it can be to help someone in need. Keep in mind that asking for and accepting help from someone is a gift to them as well as to you. There's a danger of getting caught up in your own world failing to see how your actions influence those around you causing a disconnection. Being independent takes work.

Circumstances beyond our control can make us dependent on others. When we feel independent we see the world through the eyes of someone without constraints forgetting there are others, whether through illness, divorce or job loss who may need help to get by. When I was going thru my transition I had to lean on my sister as my support system, because I was in a depressed state I wasn't able mentally to be that strong independent person.

It's complacent, when you have felt independent; able to care for yourself and do whatever you choose all your life. It's a shock when that gets taken away from you even when you know it's temporary. It turns your world upside. People will also make assumptions about someone who's self-sufficient and won't offer help as readily or invite involvement because they think you don't want or need it leaving you feeling alone and having to ask for it. Sometimes, the one who is always the strong one needs to replenish their strength thru someone else, when they are drained. One person can accomplish a lot in life but there is power in unity. Independence is a gift but like everything else in life going to the extreme is counter effective. You don't realize the value of independence until you lose it, nor do you realize the gifts that come from engaging with others more and asking for help. Our culture values independence. We all gain when we shift our value to interdependence, when you are mutually reliant on each other. Interdependence is the idea that you as a person depend on other people for certain things. The same is true of families, towns, and even countries. The people who use their own hands to make everything they could ever want are rare these days. More common are people, who get different things from different people.

What Is Marriage?

So far we have discussed the act of independency and its affect on relationships. Lets take a look at why some say they are not married where being independent is not completly the whole reason why. Does God truly give you the desires of your heart? As a single have you ever asked the question, "If God gives me the desires of my heart, why am I still single?" Of all the questions I've been asked, this is probably the number one question. To understand this Scripture fully, it's important to put it in context.

"Trust in the LORD and do good; dwell in the land and enjoy safe pasture. Delight yourself in the LORD and he will give you the desires of your heart. Commit your way to the LORD; trust in him and he will do this: He will make your righteousness shine like the dawn, the justice of your cause like the noonday sun. Be still before the LORD and wait patiently for him" **(Psalm 37:5-7).**

Today, if you're struggling in your singleness, don't lose heart. These verses are key in helping you with your frustration of being single. Is your delight, your joy, in the Lord? This is vital for anyone to have true joy. The first 20 years of my adult life I put much of my joy in my boyfriends. My mood swings went from high to low depending on how a relationship was going. I later realized my joy was in a man, not in my relationship with the Lord. Our delight must be first in the Lord. It must be priority in our lives.

Second, are you "trusting in Him and doing good?"
Countless singles are doing their own thing, not trusting
in Him, much less doing good. Many are dating
unbelievers and choosing an impure lifestyle.
God says, "Blessed are the pure in heart, for they shall
see God" **(Matthew 5:8)**. If you want a blessed life, then
it must be a pure life. Later in these verses David writes,
"Commit your way to the Lord and trust in Him."
Continue to tell the Lord you want His way, not your
way. Never ever try to make a relationship happen. Far
too many people are doing this only to end up
heartbroken. We are also commanded to be still and to
wait on Him. Waiting is a difficult thing to do. At times it
gets long and it may seem too hard. Often we cannot
endure the waiting and we rush into a wrong marriage.
Wait. Keep waiting. Don't rush.

If you are truly delighting in Him, trusting in Him,
committing your way to Him, and waiting on Him, yes,
He will give you the desires of your heart. Scripture tells
us He will. But God's timing may not be your timing.
Have you come to the end of yourself and truly asked the
Lord to change your desires if they're not His desires? I
have done this in my own life. Today I'm still single, but
never thought I could be happy if I was not married. My
desires have changed. If the Lord brings me a husband,
then I feel quite sure my desires will change again.

The key to the Christian life, single or married, is trusting
and obeying. How very, very true the famous hymn
writer was when he penned the words "Trust and obey
for there is no other way to be happy in Jesus but to trust

and obey" I'm not saying it's easy. I'm not saying there will not be times of loneliness. I'm not saying that you don't ever wonder why you're still single. But I am saying you will never ever be sorry for trusting, obeying, and waiting on the Lord. Does God give you the desires of your heart? Yes, and even more. It may be different plans or desires than you ever thought you wanted. He has extraordinary plans when you simply put Him first in your life.

God wants to show through the church that all the prejudices against God and man can be dissolved and overcome through Christ. "New" implies freshness, rather than from the point of time. It is part of the different perspective one receives upon conversion. Doing what He says to do is new for a convert because it means operating from the perspective of cooperation rather than competition. It is a new thing for a convert to show love, which is the exercising or the application of God's Word.

There are those that say they may not be completely happy with who they are and would like some time to explore what they have to offer to the world. They still haven't found the one for them and will not settle just because the clock is ticking. Marriage is not a game and they will not play for a proposal, because they don't want a divorce after six months. Marriage is not associated to a certain age or a certain culture. My heart may be still healing from a past relationship. Many say they haven't found that special person they can see themselves with for the rest of their lives or still can't picture who they want next to them on their wedding day. Because they still haven't found the one who falls in love with all their scars.

Even though your parents may want grandkids and they want to make sure someone out there will take care of you, it's not for everybody. Some are still not ready for all of that. Some say they will not live with someone before they connect with them emotionally, intellectually, and master the art of their imperfections. The hook-up culture has ruined it for all of us. We are strong enough to live by ourselves-at least for now. As much as they may hate loneliness, it still gives them the sweetness and safety some long for.

I personally refuse to believe that all marriages are hard and love is dead. I am not willing to compromise my soul to please society. I'm more concerned about the marriage than the white dress and the wedding day. Been there done that. I still want to be able to dance and write and laugh and sing and I don't want anyone to suppress all of that. God is still finishing my story before he lets someone else read it. My friends are not more "aggressive" or "smarter" than I am for settling down early; they simply want different things in life than I do. I am not too "demanding" or too "picky"; I am just trying to find the one who makes me smile and can keep me smiling, Because I once was a hopeless romantic, now I just believe in love.

I've always been a big fan of marriage. Scientific research has long promoted the benefits of being married, from happiness to better health. Researchers at Michigan State University recently conducted a study which suggested that married men have more advantages than their bachelor bros. "Just being in a well-adjusted, long-term romantic partnership with someone may be the underlying mechanism," says one of the authors of the study.

Demographers at Cornell University published a study last year which cited that "fear of divorce" was the reason why couples don't get married. According to the research: "Among cohabitating couples, more than two-thirds of the study's respondents admitted to concerns about dealing with the social, legal, emotional and economic consequences of a possible divorce." Another reason why couples aren't getting married may be explained by the rise of "stay over relationships," or relationships where parties sleep over at each other's homes a few nights a week but have the option to return to their own homes. As you can imagine, stay over relationships are popular among collegiate 20-somethings, "who are committed, but not interested in cohabiting."

After interviewing college-educated adults in committed, exclusive relationships; "As soon as couples live together, it becomes more difficult to break up. At that point, they have probably signed a lease, bought a couch and acquired a dog, making it harder to disentangle their lives should they break up. Staying over doesn't present those entanglements." Also, stay over couples appeared to be content, but weren't necessarily on the road to marriage or moving in together.

Multiple studies make it seem like living together is equivalent to marriage, which doesn't exactly make me feel better. After all, if they are so similar – why is it so difficult to cross the barrier into marriage territory? Well, it's not difficult for everyone, apparently. Modern women, like me, do want to get married. For 37 percent of women 18 to 34 (compared to 28 percent in 1997), having a successful marriage is one of the most important things in their life, according to the Pew Research Center.

Men, on the other hand, are on marriage strike. The number of men who want to get married dropped from 35 percent to 29 percent. So there it is. Finally, the million dollar question: Why don't men want to get married? (Or in my case, why have they never thought about it?) Some anti-feminist blame women for men not wanting to be married. They explain that "men have nowhere to go" because women are angry and defensive. Women have "been raised to think of men as the enemy," they believe. "Armed with this new attitude, women pushed men off their pedestals and climbed up to take what they were taught to believe was rightfully theirs."

Ladies Home Journal also tackled the question. A few reasons why young men wait (… and wait) to get married are: Men get laid anyway. Men get the benefits of having a wife when they cohabitate. "They also view living together as less risky than marriage. At the same time, the men in the study like the convenience of having a regular sex partner." Men want to wait to have kids – they don't care that their partners have their own biological clocks. Men are scared of change and compromise.

Certain blogs have theories on why men are scared of marriage. Among other things, they blame the onslaught of anti-marriage (pro bachelordom) propaganda by media, the financial burden of every girl's dream wedding, fear of divorce, and the sharing of power over one's man cave. I stop and think: Is any of this helpful? Not really. While it's all certainly interesting, these are all opinions from other people about other people – who are not in my relationship.

I finally realize that the only person who really does know the answer is me and my partner. I don't know what's going to happen – perhaps, we'll head down the altar after all, or maybe we'll part ways and he'll become the subject of a very depressing blog entry. All I know is that I am glad I brought up the conversation. I had to do it. At the end of the day, marriage or not, I have to look out for myself and my own wellbeing – because no one else is going to do that for me.

Steve Harvey agrees:
"Your objective is to avoid being on a string. The first step, I think, is to get over the fear of losing a man by confronting him. Just stop being afraid, already. The most successful people in this world recognize that taking chances to get what they want is much more productive than sitting around being too scared to take a shot. The same philosophy can be applied to dating: if

putting your requirements on the table means you risk him walking away, it's a risk you have to take. Because that fear can trip you up every time; all too many of you let the guy get away with disrespecting you, putting in minimal effort and holding on to the commitment to you because you're afraid he's going to walk away and you'll be alone again. And we men? We recognize this and play on it, big time." - From Act Like a Lady, Think Like a Man

Sanctified Answer to Why Am I Not Married:

If you have indeed been single a while my dear sister. First I think it is very important that you don't get anxious and worried about the fact that you are not married yet. Anxiety and worry create fear and confusion. Anxious, worried single adults are prime targets for desperation and deception.

Remember God knows how old you are and He is not concerned in the least that you are 43 or 50 and still not married. **Jeremiah 29:11** says I have not lost sight of My plan for you and the Lord says, and it is your welfare I have in mind, not your undoing, for you too, I have a destiny and a hope. God has not forgotten about you or your desire for a marriage partner. Relax! As to whether you should be more aggressive and use a computerized dating service or invite a man out. **Proverbs 18:22 says**: He who finds a wife finds what is good and receives favor from the LORD. This passage seems to indicate that pursuit of a marriage partner should be initiated by the man. If you are interested in receiving a marriage partner from God, you as a Christian single women should not be aggressive in your pursuit of men, but trust God to bring to you the man he wants you to have in your season.

Proverbs 3:5-6 says: Trust in the LORD with all your heart and lean not on to your own understanding; in all your ways acknowledge him, and he will direct your path.

That does not mean you should not attend events where available single men are in attendance, but you should not be aggressive in your approach to them. Let God orchestrate it for you. He orchestrated it for Rebecca and she got Isaac, he orchestrated for Rahab and she got Salmon and he orchestrated for Ruth and she got Boaz.

Isaiah 26:3 tells us we can have perfect peace, if we keep our minds on the Lord not on getting married. Your heavenly Father knows what you have need of.

How Can We Return To Our First Love?

How can I return to my "first love" for the Lord? Rekindling Your "First Love" for the Lord we must remember to repent, and do the "first works" When a person receives Christ as his Savior, he experiences the delight of "first love" for the Lord. God's Spirit witnesses with his spirit that he is a child of God **The Spirit Himself bears witness with our spirit that we are children of God, (Romans 8:16),** and this newfound relationship brings great joy and freedom.

Unfortunately, many Christians fall away from this first love. When a believer does not depend on God to meet his daily needs, his love for God grows cold. Jesus addressed this issue when He spoke to the church of Ephesus. Jesus said: **"I have somewhat against thee, because thou hast left thy first love. Remember therefore from whence thou art fallen, and repent, and do the first works . . or else I will come unto thee quickly, and will remove thy candlestick out of his place, except thou repent ." (Revelation 2:4–5).** If you find yourself in this position, ask God to have mercy on you and to rekindle your love for Him.

Remember, Repent, and Do the "First Works" Recalling your salvation experience and your first love for the Lord can help you recognize changes that have developed in your relationship with God since then. Do you have a greater or weaker sense of your need for God now? Are you cooler toward God and less passionate about spiritual things than you once were?

If so, repent of your indifference toward God. Repentance involves a change of mind, heart, and direction. Forsake the thoughts, attitudes, and actions that have drawn your attention away from wholehearted love for God. Receive God's forgiveness, and renew your commitment to do the "first works" of your faith.

Understand the Purpose of Doing the "First Works" In Revelation 2:5, the word first means "foremost (in time, place, order or importance)," and the word works is defined as "toil (as an effort or occupation)." In other words, if you find that you have left your first love for the Lord, get your priorities back in order and do the most important things.

Obviously, from the definition of work, this involves effort; it is not something that happens without effort on your part or without grace on God's part. First works could refer to many "important efforts," worship, prayer, Bible study, giving, fasting, and service to others. Each of these activities is designed to deepen your intimate relationship with God.

Worship
One of the ways that we bring glory to God and cultivate our love for Him is by worshiping Him. Take time to ponder God. Consider His acts in creation and in the circumstances of your life. Adore Him. Sing praises to Him. Bless His holy name.
"One thing have I desired of the Lord, that will I seek after; that I may dwell in the house of the Lord all the

days of my life, to behold the beauty of the Lord, and to inquire in his temple" (Psalm 27:4).

Prayer

Each aspect of prayer is designed to remind you of your dependence on God:

-Petitions bring to mind the spiritual, emotional, and physical needs that you face each day. Your resources cannot meet these needs—you need God's intervention.

-Requests reveal your motives. Are you seeking to advance God's kingdom, or are you attempting to build your own kingdom (i.e., satisfying selfish desires)?

-Confession recognizes your unworthiness before a holy God and His immeasurable mercy and love for you, His child.

-Thanksgiving reflects an understanding of your dependence on God as you thank Him for meeting specific needs.

-Intercession is the means by which you share the needs of others before God's throne.

"Be anxious for nothing, but in everything by prayer and supplication, with thanksgiving, let your requests be made known to God; and the peace of God, which surpasses all understanding, will guard your hearts and minds through Christ Jesus." (Philippians 4:6–7).

Reading, studying, memorizing, and meditating on Scripture causes you to grow in grace and in the knowledge of your Lord Jesus Christ. **As "newborn babes" you are to "desire the sincere milk of the word, that ye may grow thereby" (I Peter 2:2).** The awareness of your need for God will fuel your desire for His Word.

Studying the Bible may lead to discouragement as you learn about God's holiness and how far short you fall from His perfection. God commands us to be holy as He is holy. **For this is the will of God, that by doing good you may put to silence the ignorance of foolish men— as free, yet not using liberty as a cloak for vice, but as bondservants of God. (I Peter 1:15–16),** but instead of fostering discouragement, this understanding can create a deepening sense of need before your loving, merciful Father.

But God demonstrates His own love toward us, in that while we were still sinners, Christ died for us. (Romans 5:8),

For He knows our frame; He remembers that we are dust. (Psalm 103:14), and

Therefore, my beloved, as you have always obeyed, not as in my presence only, but now much more in my absence, work out your own salvation with fear and trembling; for it is God who works in you both to will and to do for His good pleasure. (Philippians 2:12– 13.)

Giving

Jesus instructed His disciples, **"Freely ye have received, freely give" (Matthew 10:8).** Generosity offsets the compulsion to be "rich, and increased with goods"

Because you say, 'I am rich, have become wealthy,

and have need of nothing'—and do not know that you
are wretched, miserable, poor, blind, and naked.
(Revelation 3:17),** A state of life that can cool your love
for God. Giving a tithe (ten percent of your income) or
more is not simply a way to financially support the
Church—it is a regular reminder that all you have
belongs to God. **Command those who are rich in this
present age not to be haughty, nor to trust in
uncertain riches but in the living God, who gives us
richly all things to enjoy. Let them do good, that they
be rich in good works, ready to give, willing to share,
storing up for themselves a good foundation for the
time to come, that they may lay hold on eternal life.
(1Timothy 6:17–19)**

Fasting

Fasting effectively demonstrates the reality that **life does
not consist of the things you possess** as it talks about in
(Luke 12:15) and **So He humbled you, allowed you to
hunger, and fed you with manna which you did not
know nor did your fathers know, that He might make
you know that man shall not live by bread alone; but
man lives by every word that proceeds from the
mouth of the Lord (Deuteronomy 8:3)** and deepens
your awareness of spiritual, mental, and emotional needs.

Serving

Ask the Lord to give you attentiveness to His voice as He
brings needs to your attention and directs you to meet
them—in His strength, with His love, and for His glory.
As you serve in His name, you will know the joy of the
Lord, which is your strength. **Then he said to them,**

"Go your way, eat the fat, drink the sweet, and send portions to those for whom nothing is prepared; for this day is holy to our Lord. Do not sorrow, for the joy of the Lord is your strength." (Nehemiah 8:10.)

If you have left your first love for the Lord, remember, repent, and return to the first works of your faith. May God rekindle your love for Him!

God is asking each of us to do the same thing He asked of the church at Ephesus. He is asking us to remember where we once were. He is counseling us to come back to the passion we once had for Jesus.

Go back to that moment when you first met Jesus. Remember the love you felt, the stirring in your heart, the adoration you had for the Savior? Do you remember how grateful you were for the forgiveness of sins? Do you remember how at that moment nothing else mattered, only Jesus?

God wants you and me to go back and remember that moment in time. And having that in our memory He wants us to return. He wants us to come back to Him; to come back to our first love, to the place and time in our lives to where He was everything to us. That's where He wants us.

Personal Perceptions:

This is my perception of Independence: Like anything applied properly is a good thing, but not so good when implemented improperly. I would liken independence to a hammer. A hammer can drive nails, bend hard metals and break or smash other materials.

A woman's independence is her beauty; her crown of Glory. There is a story in Hebraic writings that tell of such a woman. This woman is said to rise early in the morning to tend to her home and then her family. After which she turns her attention to her Limited Liability Company (LLC) and weaves exquisite fabrics and clothing. She is the Vera Wang of her day! She knows that the strength of her independence is to serve/care for her husband, her family and to love her God.

What happens when that same independence is used selfishly or as a hammer taken to let's say glass!! Is this woman's first priority to her husband/family? Or is she fiercely independent and clings to her independence as who she is more so than what she does? Does her Independence serve her? Or is it the other way around? Even a woman without her own husband and children can fall prey to the dark side of independence. Just examine her personal life. Who does she invest in? Can she be found at the children's hospital reading stories to sickly children? Caring for the elderly in her neighborhood? Volunteering down at the youth center?

So, maybe good independence and great character go hand in hand? As a man I have always admired a woman who could do for herself but always appreciated having someone around to share the load and not have to be so independent. I often tell women (while I'm holding open a door or helping to carry heavy/or not so heavy items) that, If a man wants to help! Let him! It does not mean that he thinks you can't handle it; It only means that he feels that you shouldn't't have to when he's around.

**Anonymous

This is my perception of Independence: Independence to me means something deeper than the physical. I used to believe Independence meant your own car and home, or not needing anyone else for your material needs or wants. I had my first encounter with independence at the age of 17. I moved out of my mom's house at that time with a full time job and a vision out of this world. Even with the perks and responsibilities of adulthood, I didn't't feel independent. It was almost like I still needed something.

So, after a year of independence, at the age of 18. I moved back to New York where I found my daughters father and we lived as a family for five years. No one paid our bills; we didn't't have to answer to anyone. it was a great feeling to know that this is what we had accomplished. Yet and still I was missing something and I had to search for that so I moved from New York to

Texas. Once again alone doing things by myself but now with my child. I was more independent than I had ever been in my whole life. This came with more stress. I confided in friends and family. I buried my life into other people's priorities just to fill that sense of being in charge. All that got me was involved in everyone else's problems without solving mine. I got tired, tired of the chase for happiness, purpose, for self-independence. It wasn't until 10 years after that pivotal point in my teenage years, that I truly found independence.

I came closer to finding that when I learned to release and let go. I let go of my mistakes and blame. I let go of the people hanging on to me, hindering me from growth. I started to move in different ways than I had ever moved and not answering those calls I would once answer. Then one day it happened. I was speaking to the universe, completely open and transparent in heart and spirit, at that time I asked for strength and happiness. I couldn't't pull the strength I needed from family and nothing seemed to make me happy. But, when my spirit cried out, my whole entire world was changed. I immediately got strength.

All of a sudden the options that I had become plentiful and clear to me. I learned that independence is a spiritual and very lonely journey that you embark on. It doesn't't mean being able to afford your habits of nice cars and restaurants. It means the ability to pick yourself up and make a way. Being strong for yourself even when you're at that point that you've been crying for 3 days and no one else is there for you. Independence, means depending on self, mind, body and spirit. Once you master independence of this caliber you become so in tuned with all the spiritual aspects of this reality and many others.

**Anonymous

This is my perception of Independence: Independence to me came about when I finally realized that I can do whatever that is positive for me and my family alone and with Gods guidance and blessings. I've been through hell and back. When I continuously worried about what people thought of me. Having that disability gave me the most negative reaction, which was followed by a pattern of destructional behaviors. And what I learned from this pattern is that u cannot ever please anyone but yourself first. And once I grasped that reality then the real understanding of independence kicked in and it was a blessing, a blessing from God.

It affected my relationships with men as being very distrustful and Leary. You see women have made excuses for their men`s actions especially when their hearts and children are involved. And now that I have experienced marriage and the love thing with the men I chose to be in my life It was always letting me down in the end. So as far as a relationship, yes I am going to give it another try but it happens or it don't I have chosen to continue to be the woman that I have become.

**Anonymous

This is my perception: I feel being independent can be a Good and bad thing. Being independent allows me the Peace of not having to depend on anyone. I make sure I handle everything that needs to be taken care of in fear of having to ask someone. The bad side of it is, when I really need help, I will not ask for it. I would rather go without, than to have someone talk bad or throw it in my face.

**Anonymous

This is my perception of independence: Well, I think that having the ability to extend the feelings of ones purpose or conducting exactly how everything at that junction is part of independence. I don't see it as a curse because having the right to make bad decisions can only come as a learning mechanism, and therefore it's most seemingly is redundant. You heard of the phrase, what goes around comes around? Well having independence is the best part of waking up to new avenues, freely. Sometimes people get away with too much when it comes down to independence. That's what I would call a curse, and you would think being practical is obligational to being fairly correspondent to right and wrong. Its almost outrageous to point out the sweet science of independence, Its always going to be compromised.

**Anonymous

This is my perception of Life, Love Independence and everything in between. I remember when I was married and committed in a long-term relationship I was both happy and miserable at the same time. I was married twice and both of my wives did not appreciate who I was in their lives. They both took me for granted; took advantage of my meekness, genuine love, compassion and goodness; they both misused and abused my trust. They both ended up regretting it after losing me in their lives.

I remember being with my first wife for a short two and the half years and when I found out she was cheating I left. My second marriage lasted for almost 19 years, but I went through hell and back. I admit when I was dating her I had two girlfriends and was not fully divorced from my first wife. My second wife was going through a divorce too at the time so I was not really sure we were going to end up together. She was flip flopping back and forth between her first husband and me, but from her perspective I was a cheater. After all of the drama between us I had decided to be fully committed to her. We moved in together and were eventually married. Once I made that decision I was committed and never cheated but every time we had an agreement of disagreement she would accuse me of being a liar and a cheater and she never trusted me no matter how hard or how much I did to prove to her that I was a good man and a faithful husband. I was accused of cheating every four months, which made my life miserable. I did have some happy times and we did have a lot of fun traveling and raising children together, but she never got pass the fact that I was with someone else. She would never look at her situation and why things turned out the way they did. But I found out that was her own insecurity due to the fact that she was cheating with both men and women and was saying to herself, "why is he not cheating on me since I am doing it to him?"

I have found that marriage flourishes when the couple works together as a team, when both husband and wife decide that working together is more important. Good marriages have great communication, respect and genuine equal love. A good marriage is hard work, which requires honesty, undying commitment and selfless love at the center of it all. I at one time loved my wife whole-heartedly and always considered how she would feel in every decision that I made. I was giving her more than half my pay check and all of the extra money I made when I had a second job and she never saw the fact that I was worth anything to her. That women abused my kindness every chance she got and was very mean to me about how I was as a parent and a provider. I was abused verbally and physically on occasion.

The beginning of the end was when I lost my job and she became unhappy because we did not have all of the money we had as a couple. So she started to cheat blatantly with another women and then with another man. When she asked for a divorce, It was a blessing in disguise. I was sad to the fact that my marriage was over with, and how she asked for a divorce was on Christmas day, and how she threw me out of the house that I paid the mortgage on for almost 19 years. But when I think about it and really evaluate it was a blessing.

I learned to be single. At first it was very hard to be by myself. I had to learn to sleep by myself and be comfortable by myself. Once I got used to being single I learned a lot. For one thing I can travel when and where I want. I can flirt with out consequence. I can do whatever I wanted without my partner saying that was selfish. In my two break ups I have learned that even though it hurt to lose my wives in losing them they did not appreciate me in the first place and respect me enough. It was an asset it was not a loss.

I am not ashamed of what I been through I wear my divorces as a badge of honor because I learned a great deal about myself and how to overcome. In being single and Independent now I have learned to love myself and be independent. I have been divorced now for five years and I had plenty of time to reflect on life. Self-love is a real thing and honestly it's more reliable and fulfilling than a lot of romantic relationships. But being single affords you a unique opportunity: you get to really find out that you are. The good, the bad, the indifferent, are all lay bare. Your strengths, weaknesses and insecurities exposed. Embrace the solitude and vow to learn and uncover everything about you. My last relationship caused me a lot of mental and physical health issues, which I am still trying to bounce back from. Mentally I am fine but physically I have aged a great deal. I am using this time to heal, to nourish my body, exercise and I have achieved a peace of mind I did not have when I was with someone. Do not get me wrong I am not anti-marriage or am I anti-relationship I am just saying you need time to yourself. Especially after a break up, it's easy to enjoy being alone once I realized that doing so gave me more freedom to do the things I actually want to do. Once I was alone, the only person's happiness I had to worry about in that moment was my own. So often we feel we the need to get validation from our friends and family before we take action. We constantly look to other people for advice on what we should do next. In being by myself I learned to trust my instincts and make decisions without any third party validation. For me being single and Independent is a Blessing.

**Anonymous

This is my perception of Independence: it can be either good or bad. It pretty much falls into the taboo of being too confident which can possible lead to arrogance. There has to be some form of balance when looking at independence. For myself, I have been known to be too independent which hasn't always worked for me. Actually, majority of the time it doesn't work for me. I have had to learn how to balance when to be independent and when not to be. There is nothing wrong with asking for help. If God intended on us never needing help, He would've just made one person on the entire planet. So, I will say, have discernment of when to be independent and when to ask for help

**Anonymous

This is my perception of Independence: I have always been a leader and very independent from a early age. I remember at the age of 5 one Christmas when i got my first green machine. All the kids were playing outside with their new toys and bikes. I had all the kids from the neighborhood line up their bikes with mine and charged .10 cents so the kids would be able to ride on all the bikes and my Green machine that they didn't get and of course i kept the money. My mother said she knew right then that i had the entrepreneur spirit. God knows what you need when you need it. I have always treated women like queens, i love hard and I'm happy when my woman is happy. I don't mind my woman being independent but I'm a nurturer, by being raised by my mother and grandmother so with me she will never feel like she has to be independent. There are some guys that see a woman that's independent and they prey on that, they see all this promise in her and they try to capitalize on her weakness even though they are capable of getting their own but they rather her hold it down and they just chill. Those are not men. All my relationships with women that ended which was not a lot, always ended good and we remained friends because they knew I was a good dude.

**Anonymous

This is my perception of Independence, whether it's a curse or a blessing.   There are many factors that play a part in being Independent, some negative and some positive. Independence within itself is not a bad thing;

however when a person shows themselves to be very independent sometimes it can bring negative feedback. What I mean by saying this is simply that when a person shows themselves to be a strong individual this can cause others around them to hold back on putting their best performance forward because they are leaning on you. They have become accustomed to the "WHY SHOULD I WORRY. THEY WILL GET THE JOB DONE "attitude.

They know that no matter what you are the one who makes sure everything is done and taken care of. You are the one who's going to double check a project to be sure everything is exactly as it should be. You are the one who's going to make sure every bill is paid even if it means working more than one job. It's unfortunate that many times because of your independence you will find yourself standing alone because you are the one who carries all the weight whether it's on your job, in your home or in a relationship.

As I previously stated independence within itself is not a bad thing. It's an honorable achievement and something everyone should aspire to. Independence not abused is beautiful. It shows Integrity, good character and trust. This is when the blessings of being independent come in. This is where entrepreneurs and CEOs are born and recognized as great achievers.

**Anonymous

This is my perception of Independence whether it's a blessing or a curse: Being independent is a blessing not a curse, it teaches responsibility and enhances growth. When one is independent they are not lazy, independent people like to work earning their own money, not asking for handouts. They learn to love themselves being whole and not needy, they are not afraid to try new things, explore and blossom. Most Independent people become entrepreneurs.

Independence promotes growth, strength, and freedom. Speaking from experience, a person who has been independent for quite a long time. I learned to make my own decisions, (calling the shots) I learned to figure out situations on my own, hold down an apartment, job, bills you name it; I learned to rely on my own thoughts getting things done. Independent people do not need much assistance unless they ask for it. They're not afraid to try something challenging. Being independent allows one to think swiftly without a second thought. An independent person will finds ways to put the pieces back together and keep stuff from falling apart, getting the job done.

This is the nature of independence. Independence can become a curse only when the help of others is not utilized. We all need help every now and then, if not independence will turn into control, a place that should not be occupied. A controlling character is not healthy due to one taking charge, with little or no correction. If we find ourselves not taking advice, tending to put others down, this is a problem. Everyone needs a balance, overly strong in any character can be dangerous. Again Independence is good because it shows one is able to conquer situations with no fear. As individuals allowing independence to override others views, thinking they are better than the next person, shows bad character traits.

Independence is not a curse as long as it's used in the right perspective.

Peace,

**Anonymous

Meet the Author

Sonya Lyons

You know my name. Not my story.
You see my smile. Not my pain.
You notice my cuts. Not my scars.
You can read my lips. Not my mind.

Sonya Lyons is a true New Yorker, born and raised in The Bronx. As a teenage mom she learned how to survive in the tough city using what she had: her wit and good looks. It is her instinct to survive that has helped her to keep it all together through lean economic times and during her lifelong quest to find "the right man". Through lack and gain - joy and pain Sonya Lyons has fought to maintain her walk with The Lord but not always succeeding.

In March of 1993 she was introduced to the Holy Spirit shortly after taking the Right Hand of Fellowship at Bethel Gospel Assembly (Harlem NYC) under the Pastorship of the Late Bishop Ezra N. Williams. It was during her very first all night prayer; while tarrying for the Holy Ghost, surrounded by the praying church Mothers that she suddenly felt His presence. So frightened by the experience, she stopped tarrying altogether. A decision that would alter the direction of her life for many years to come. Sonya lacked the understanding that the whole point of tarrying and waiting was to invite Him deeper into her life.

After the birth of her son Sonya left The Big City and headed for Atlanta Georgia, where she now resides with her family. Through all of her trials, tribulations and attempts to satisfy a deep inner void with the right relationship, she finally realized that the only person who can fill that void in her life was God. And so it was not until she gave herself completely to God's will that she found peace. In addition she also discovered her great affinity toward literature.

As we live and navigate our way through this thing called life, we are filled with wonderful memories, lessons that we have learned and friends that we have made along the way but, in many cases we have also been left with many hurts and scars.

Sonya Lyons in choosing to give her all to Christ also chose to overcome those hurts. In her book "Why Am I Not Married? Independence, A Blessing or a Curse?" Minister and Author Sonya Lyons shares her struggles and victories in her pilgrims journey toward the Cross. She takes an honest look at why we as women will abandon our "good sense" just to have a man in our lives! In other words "We know better! So why don't we do better!". While on the one hand, life is about learning from our successes and mistakes but, on the other hand if we choose to truly love God making Him first and then learn to really love and appreciate our own worth...we'll maybe then we won't have quite so many mistakes to learn from!

In the process of writing her book, Miss Lyons realized that writing out her experiences (journaling) was very therapeutic. Journaling helps us to see in black and white just what kind of person we were and what we have become. The love of Christ has helped those scars to disappear. So - Come! See a man who knows all that I have done! **John 4:29.** So now she wishes to share the knowledge she received with the world, with hopes it may help someone. It may not be for everybody, but it's for somebody.

The Lion of the Tribe of Judah fundamental passage (
**Rev 5:5). And one of the elders saith unto me, Weep
not: behold, the Lion of the tribe of Judah, the Root of
David, hath prevailed to open the book, and to loose
the seven seals thereof.**
God had revealed that the ruler would be like a lion, an
offspring of Judah **(Gen 49:9-10; Ps. 60:7).** Jesus was
born in the line of Judah **(Mat. 1:2-3; Luke 3:33; Heb.
7:14)**. Although Reuben was the firstborn, due to his sin
and the sins of his brothers, the right of kingly rule fell to
Judah. The Lion of Judah is the symbol of the Hebrew
tribe of Judah (the Jewish tribe). According to the Torah,
the tribe consists of the descendants of Judah, the fourth
son of Jacob. ... The Lion of Judah is also mentioned in
the Book of Revelation, as a term representing Jesus,
according to Christian theology.
Lyons is a surname with a variety of origins, from
England, Ireland, Scotland, or perhaps France. The
English surname Lyons can be traced back to the Norman
French, when it was introduced after the Norman
Conquest in 1066. It could originally have been an
individual's nickname, from the Old French lion,
signifying a brave or fierce warrior, or even an
individual's name like Leo.[1] Alternately it could be a
locational name from the small town of Lyons-la-Forêt in
Normandy or less likely the central French town of
Lyons. It is believed that both of these towns derive their
names from old Celtic tongues spoken in Gaul – see
Lugdunum (Lyon), and Lyons-la-Forêt.
The Surnames of Ireland[2] by Edward MacLysaght
describes Lyons having its roots as a surname from the
County Galway name of Ó Laighin, meaning grey. It

could also be a variant of the Irish Ó Liatháin of County Cork.[3] It may also be a variant of the typically Scottish surname Lyon.

Although most Hebrew and Greek words for lion are used in a figurative sense, nevertheless we can draw a number of inferences regarding the perceived characteristics and behavior of literal lions. They are, among other things, strong **(Pr 30:30)**, especially in their teeth **(Job 4:10)** and paws **(1 Sam 17:37)**, fearless **(Prov 28:1 ; 30:30)**, stealthy **(Psalm 17:12)**, frightening **(Ezra 19:7 ; Hosea 11:10 ; Amos 3:8)**, destructive **(1 Sam 17:34** ; Micah 5:8), and territorially protective **(Isa 31:4)**. Yet for all its seeming autonomy, the lion is ultimately dependent on God **(Job 38:39-40); Psalm 104:21)**, answerable to him **(Job 4:10),** and subdued in the millennial age **(Isa 11:6-7)**.

The many notable qualities of the lion are often applied figuratively in a variety of ways to individuals and nations. The king is frightening in his anger **(Prov 19:12 ; 20:2)**, the soldier courageous **(2 Sam 17:10)**, national leaders vicious **(Ezek 22:25 ; Zeph 3:3)**, enemy nations destructive **(Isa 5:29 ; Jer 2:15)** and protective of their conquests **(Isa 5:29)**, and personal enemies stealthy in their pursuit to **harm (Psalm 10:9 ; 17:12)**.

God is described with a number of leonine features. He is strong **(Isa 38:13)**, fearless in protecting his own **(Isa 31:4)**, stealthy in coming upon his prey **(Jer 49:19 ; Hosea 13:7)**, frightening **(Hosea 11:10 ; Amos 3:8)**, and destructive **(Jer 25:38 ; Lam 3:10 ; Hosea 5:14 ; 13:8).** In am 3:8 "The Lion" even appears as a title for God.

www.ingramcontent.com/pod-product-compliance
Lightning Source LLC
Chambersburg PA
CBHW072201090426
42740CB00012B/2346